T0301730

ORGANIZATIONAL COMMITMENT
The Case of Unrewarded Behavior

ORGANIZATIONAL COMMITMENT
The Case of Unrewarded Behavior

Aviad Bar-Haim
Open University of Israel

World Scientific

W JERSEY · LONDON · SINGAPORE · BEIJING · SHANGHAI · HONG KONG · TAIPEI · CHENNAI · TOKYO

Published by

World Scientific Publishing Co. Pte. Ltd.

5 Toh Tuck Link, Singapore 596224

USA office: 27 Warren Street, Suite 401-402, Hackensack, NJ 07601

UK office: 57 Shelton Street, Covent Garden, London WC2H 9HE

Library of Congress Cataloging-in-Publication Data

Names: Bar Haim, Aviad, author.

Title: Organizational commitment : the case of unrewarded behavior /
  Aviad Bar-Haim (Open University of Israel, Israel).

Description: 1 Edition. | New Jersey : World Scientific, [2019] |
  Includes bibliographical references and index.

Identifiers: LCCN 2018058237 | ISBN 9789813232150

Subjects: LCSH: Organizational commitment. | Industrial relations--History. |
  Organizational behavior--History.

Classification: LCC HF5549.5.M63 B364 2019 | DDC 302.3/5--dc23

LC record available at https://lccn.loc.gov/2018058237

British Library Cataloguing-in-Publication Data

A catalogue record for this book is available from the British Library.

Copyright © 2019 by World Scientific Publishing Co. Pte. Ltd.

For any available supplementary material, please visit
https://www.worldscientific.com/worldscibooks/10.1142/10768#t=suppl

Desk Editor: Shreya Gopi

Typeset by Stallion Press
Email: enquiries@stallionpress.com

Printed in Singapore

To my family, with endless love

Contents

Preface

I link my commitment toward this study with the personal events in my life. Such a major event in my life, as a young man, was leaving a *Kibbutz* (a collective commune) in Israel, near Jerusalem, where I was born and brought up until the age of 21. When I left, the *Kibbutz* was in trouble, socially and economically, and I did not stay there to help. Leaving a *Kibbutz* in those times was almost a traitorous act. I failed the ultimate test of commitment, namely, *staying*. My personal experience fits Rosabeth Kanter's account of the American communes in the 19th century, where a major concern of those communes was the commitment of the members to their demanding way of life. I should remember this dark side of commitment. However, in studying organizational commitment for many years, I ignored this unhappy side of commitment and followed the mainstream research in this field. This stream treats organizational commitment as a positive force of behavior if you have it. I was wrong. Organizational commitment is neither motivational nor rewarded behavior. It is something else, partly explainable, and mostly enigmatic. I need to tell a different story on organizational commitment. This is the purpose of this book.

Introduction

Commitment is something that we should not hope for or need to have. Commitment is a necessary, but neither satisfying nor desired state. Commitment is an unwelcome demand to fulfill an obligation, which often requires time, money, emotions, efforts and other valuable resources. Commitment is the opposite of love. Love is what we need. Love is the sufficient condition for a desired and satisfying state. With love, time, emotions, tangible and non-tangible resources are not wasted in vain. But love is reserved only to living entities, not for organizations.

Therefore, it is not understandable why most research literature on organizational commitment describes this phenomenon in love-like terms, such as a deep affective identification and internalization of organizational goals and norms. It is sensible that some managers would wish these love-like feelings of employees toward their workplace for good reasons or selfish interests. But it is unclear why such wishful thinking is enhanced by social scientists for several decades. This unique epistemological phenomenon is found only in management studies, such as organizational behavior. In other disciplines of the social sciences, the meaning of commitment is totally different.

In sociology, commitment is a mechanism to preserve communities or to change them. In economics, commitment is the means by which past accumulation of assets is protected, or entrepreneurs' efforts to take risks and create new economic assets is evoked. In political science, commitment is a device to preserve loyalty to power holders or to create and lead toward new goals and new agendas. In psychology, commitment is either a way to protect embedded self identities or pursue new ones. In theology and cultural studies, commitment is a mechanism to protect a religion or to develop religious faiths.

In all these faculties of knowledge, commitment is a device, a process or a mechanism to secure action toward specific goals or directions in the future. The working assumption is that commitment is required to guarantee obligation fulfillment because the fulfillment of undertaken obligations and responsibilities are never secured or taken for granted. Thus, the Church cannot rely only on the faith of its believers in order to secure their religious way of life; or religious reformers and religion's creators cannot trust the enthusiasm and zealousness of their followers. Societies and communities cannot base their normative orders only on the goodwill of their citizens, or readiness to participate in social reforms or even revolutions is not sufficient to mobilize resources and energy for the change. Even ego states are not strong enough to secure embedded self-identities without commitment to preserve them. Instead, change elements of self-identity requires a lot of self-commitment. In economics, it is common knowledge that long-term behaviors such as saving require commitment, and this requirement is difficult to attain.

This side of commitment as an obligation, which has no safeguards, is well defined in the Merriam-Webster dictionary for the term COMMITMENT as follows:

A commitment to a cause is: **A**: an agreement or pledge to do something in the future; *especially*: an engagement to assume a financial obligation at a future date; **B**: something pledged; **C**: the state or an instance of being obligated or emotionally impelled.

Thus, commitment is an act of pledging or promising to fulfill an obligation to someone or something at a future date. Only the definition **C** enlarges the obligation element to an emotionally impelled cause. The application of commitment in human life is the obligation to preserve and guarantee valuable tangible and non-tangible assets in face of uncertainty and risk, and by a human behavior that functions as a safety net in the case of disastrous events.

People do not seek obligations. They are forced to fulfill obligations, for many reasons, and they may understand and accept the terms of their obligations. Simple cases of obligations are paying debts or taxes. A more complex obligation is staying with one's sick spouse without reward. The common denominator of these commitment cases is unpleasant and, in some cases, unrewarded behavior. Therefore, it is difficult to understand why commitment, which is basically a necessary but unwelcome phenomenon in everyday life and in most other disciplines of social sciences, has become a desired behavior and has been ascribed motivational power in organizational behavior and management sciences. The following historical note may partially answer how this unique epistemological disarray evolved.

Acknowledgements

This book would not be published without comments, discussions, critiques AND encouragement from several circles of colleagues, friends and academic networks.

I am grateful to my colleagues at the management and economics department and the research institute for policy studies of the Open University of Israel, who supported me and enabled me to present my ideas and empirical findings in several academic workshops and conferences.

I have many thanks to the international society for the study of work & organizational values (ISSWOV), where I had several opportunities to present my core thesis on organizational commitment as an unrewarded behavior.

I am grateful in particular to two members of ISSWOV for their encouragement: Prof. Aaron Tziner from Netanya College, Israel, and Prof. Jorge F.S. Gomes from ISEG-Lisbon Technical University, and president of ISSWOV.

Dr. Hanna Ornoy from the Open University of Israel and Ono College, Israel, was my research partner in some of my studies on organizational commitment, and I owe her for her intellectual contributions and devotion to our research project.

My friend, Ret. Colonel Eli Fischoff, who headed the Behavioral Sciences Department in the Israeli Defence Forces, helped me a lot to clarify my ideas on the uniqueness of the phenomenon of organizational commitment.

Finally, I am indebted so much to my loving and supporting late wife Rachel (Rachi) and our daughter and two sons, who never accepted my intellectual attempts to separate commitment from love.

About the Author

AVIAD BAR-HAIM is a retired professor at the Open University of Israel. He holds a doctorate in industrial sociology and organizational behavior from the Hebrew University of Jerusalem. He was the head of the OU Management and Economics Department and founded the Open University Research Institute for Policy Analysis. Before these assignments, he was the Open University's Dean for Academic Development. Among his research and teaching interests are topics in organizational behavior, human resource management and employment relations.

Chapter 1

A Chronicle of the Concept of Organizational Commitment

The use of the term organizational commitment (OC) dates back to the fifties of the 20th century. A basic concern of managers at that time was cooperation (Barnard, 1938) and willingness to stay and contribute (Simon, 1958). Both perceived the relationships between employees and employing organizations as a formal and informal (psychological and social) contract, in which loyalty and commitment are exchanged for material and non-material rewards. This approach to OC was also held by Becker (1960) in his well-known side-bet theory of OC.

One of the problematical issues at that time in the world of work was the attachment or bonding of employees and employers, in order to secure continuing production of goods and services in a prosperity era. In full-employment labor market, the workforce in the first decades after the Second World War was not easily attached to workplaces. Many of these workplaces were covered by collective bargaining regime or equivalent systems of secured labor relations, which were geared toward industrial peace. Industrial peace was a strategic keystone in attaining economic growth, and all stakeholders in labor relations, including political parties and regulators, were able to institutionalize the employment relations game, where the major players agreed to solve labor–management issues and disputes by negotiation, labor legislation and professional services. The imperative of industrial peace made organizations concerned about the attachment of their workforce. This era of the fifties and sixties of the 20th century, in a way, was a culmination of impressive scientific attainments in social sciences, since the Hawthorne experiments in Chicago in the thirties; the studies on the behavior of the American soldiers in the Second World War (compiled in the series of The American Soldier); the leadership studies in the fifties and sixties, mainly in the universities of Ohio and Michigan; the British studies at Tavistock Institute; the sociotechnical movement in England and Scandinavia in the sixties and many other breakthrough projects in organizational behavior. The common denominator in many of these studies was the spirit of the human relations movement, which inspired the intellectual efforts to explore and apply employee well-being at work.

In managing human resources (HR) of the young generation of the post-war workplaces, organizational behaviors, such as absenteeism, lateness and turnover, became a big worry to personnel managers and their higher echelons in the corporation. These behaviors emerged as an important and challenging theme in management science in general and in industrial sociology and psychology in particular. These disciplines were going to merge in this period and create a new science, organizational behavior. Scholars began to look at these behaviors, and in the discourse about attachment entered the term OC as a synonym.

From the intellectual history point-of-view, since the fifties, four views of the concept of OC emerged in the research literature.

The first view defined OC as a **calculative-instrumental** decision. In the framework of this approach, the focus of the research was on the Individual's decision to stay or leave his workplace for utilitarian reasons. Accordingly, an employee becomes committed to his workplace because of "sunk costs" (e.g., fringe benefits, salary as a function of age or tenure), and it is too costly for him or her to leave (Becker, 1960; Salancik, 1977; Blau and Boal, 1987).

The second view of OC is a **moral-normative** approach; in this case, an employee feels moral obligations to remain at his workplace. This obligation steams from the employee's support of the employing organization's goals, values and norms.

The third view defines OC as an **emotional-identification** state, "a state in which an employee identifies with a particular organization and its goals, and he/she wishes to maintain membership in the organization in order to facilitate its goals" (Blau and Boal, 1987, p. 290; Mowday *et al.*, 1979).

The fourth view defines OC as the opposite of identification, namely, **alienation** and involuntary **compliance** as forces of staying in the employing organization. Both alienation and compliance are concepts that were articulated in the works of Kelman (1958) and Etzioni (1961).

These four perspectives of OC evolved unevenly. Over the past 60 years, OC had been associated with terms such as organizational careers, organizational norms, identification, moral, work attachment, job involvement, side-bets and other related terms (Zangaro, 2001). However, the second and third views (**moral-normative** and **emotional-identification** commitment) were the most researched and discussed, whereas the definition of **calculative-instrumental** commitment was slightly changed from *side-bets* or *sunk costs* to **continuance**.

Etzioni equated commitment with attachment and identified three dimensions of it: moral involvement, calculative involvement and alienated involvement, each representing an individual's response to organizational power. Moral involvement is a positive orientation of high density and is based on an employee's internalization and identification with organizational goals. Calculative involvement is either a negative or a positive orientation of low intensity and is based on an employee receiving inducements from the organization that match his or her contributions. Alienated involvement is an intensely negative attachment to the organization, for example, the attachment of inmates in prisons, people in concentration camps and enlisted men in basic military training. These people remain in the organization only because they have no other options.

More than two decades later, Penley and Gould (1988) developed a concept of OC that corresponds closely to Etzioni's approach. Like Etzioni, Penley and Gould started with moral commitment, calculative commitment and alienated commitment. However, their research provided empirical evidence that there are only two predominant bases of OC: instrumental and affective. The instrumental view relates to the system of compensation and rewards received by an individual in return for accomplishments within the organization. The affective view relates to a person's level of emotional attachment and personal sense of obligation to fulfill duties within the organization. Thus, moral and emotional commitments are treated as affective forms of OC.

The study of Penley and Gould took many years of research and was dominated by a single-dimension approach to OC. The works of Kelman (1958) and Etzioni (1961) set up the path to view commitment as a behavior of identification. However, the most widely accepted conceptualization of OC as an emotional-identification problem was done by Mowday *et al.* (1979). This group of researchers in the seventies defined OC as the relative strength of an individual's identification with and involvement in a particular organization that is characterized by three interrelated factors: (1) a strong belief in and acceptance of the organization's goals and values, (2) a willingness to exert considerable effort on behalf of the organization and (3) a strong desire to maintain membership in the organization. This definition does not exclude the possibility that a person is committed to other aspects of the environment, such as family and social networks. Additionally, it assumes that an employee who is committed to an organization will display all three of these attributes.

In the nineties of the 20th century, an attempt to codify the research literature on OC has been made by Meyer and Allen (1997), beyond several comprehensive reviews and meta-analyses in the field. Their works and those of other scholars provided strong empirical support for the fact that OC is a multi-focus, multi-base concept. Their concept of OC consists of three components: an affective component (employee's emotional attachment to, identification with and involvement in an organization), a continuance component (commitment based on the costs that an employee bears by leaving his/her employing organization) and a normative component (an employee's feelings of obligation to remain at an organization). Meyer and Allen's model provides a comprehensive explanation to the link between employees and organizations by delineating whether an employee wants to and or needs to and or should remain at an organization.

We can see in Figure 1.1 that in the seventies of the 20th century evolved a small branch of research on OC around the notions of Exit, Voice and Loyalty. Hirschman (1970) and others (Rusbult *et al.*, 1988) noted that citizens, employees and other social groups that perceive

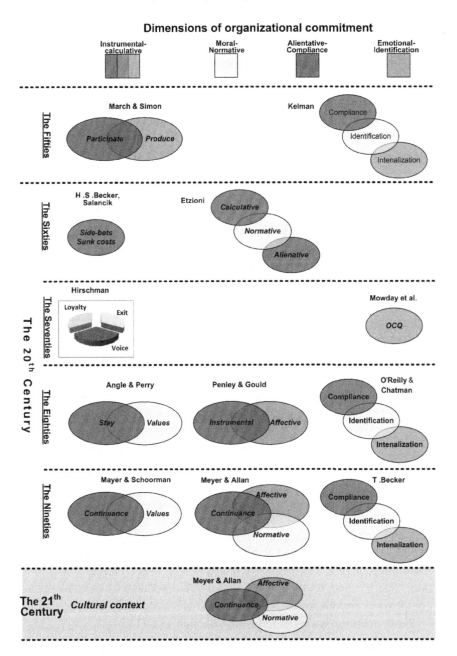

Figure 1.1. A Visual Summary of Intellectual History of the Concept of OC

deterioration in their social, work, economic or political environment can respond in one of three ways: Exit, Voice (an attempt to change the situation, sometimes by unionization) or Loyalty. The strength of Hirschman's model is behavioral: commitment is conceptualized in terms of action decisions, namely, doing Exit or Voice or Loyalty. I discuss this neglected brunch of research in the mainstream of OC in Chapter 2.

In the eighties of the 20th century, the whole picture was changing. The emergence of a new wave of globalization, this time with the driving force of high technology, mainly, information technology, had a crucial impact on the bonds between employees and their employing organizations. The drive to strengthen quality of working life, satisfaction at work and organizational democracy, as safeguards of employee retention, were replaced by polarization of the workforce in most advanced countries between large masses of low-paid workers in low-security jobs, quickly decreasing membership in labor unions and reduction in collective agreements; temporary work and agency employment and other atypical work arrangements replaced permanent employment and secured income from work. The needs and attitudes of employers were profoundly changed. Their concerns were about flexibility, not about attachment. They did not need employee commitment anymore.

The flows of production facilities and services out of local economies and local regions, and the fast mergers and acquisitions of firms and ownerships eliminated any form of long-term mutual responsibility between employers and work communities. What remained in the advanced economies was to tame the grandchildren employees of the first generation after the Second World War to adapt to the new employment relations regime.

Many of them found new industries more suitable to their occupational and career aspirations, with, apparently, less desire for attachment. However, the other masses of workers, without proper and updated human capital, mostly, young poor-educated employees, labor migrants and older lower-class workers found that OC was not reciprocated by the new breed of employing organizations.

These changes are reflected in the decline of OC novelty in research in the last two decades or so. It is not seen in the numbers of research studies. The stream of peer review publications on OC is still several dozens per year. However, no new conceptions of OC and no new research tools were developed. There is a sharp decline in OC research in Western countries, and an increased number of studies in other countries. The important added value of this shift to the field is the cultural differences of the weights of the various dimensions of OC in different countries and regions. For example, in Western countries, the affective dimension of OC is dominant, whereas in some other countries the normative dimension is prevailing.

Chapter 2

Loyalty: The Forgotten Brick in the Organizational Commitment Construct

Loyalty is a concept that has been taken for granted in the discourse of organizational commitment (OC), or even as a synonym. Apparently, the logic is: is it possible to be loyal and not committed? I arrive to this interesting question soon. But before that, let us look in the research database PROQUEST. When searching for titles of scholarly full-text academic studies containing the term **Loyalty** in their titles, we discover that until June 2016 there were 1,670 items, covering all dimensions of loyalty (interpersonal, political, in marriage, in business and so forth). However, when a search has been narrowed to the title **Loyalty And Organizational Commitment**, only three (!) articles have been found. In the EBSCO database, with 612 items with the title **Loyalty** and 213 items with the title **Organizational Commitment**, this combination has yielded three items as well.

The word loyalty is of course used numerous times in the OC literature to describe commitment. However, it is not a focal researched term there. It is not defined scientifically there, and, as a result, it is not systematically measured in the context of OC. So, the answer to the previous question is *NO*. Loyalty is not a synonym of OC. It has not even been a concept important enough to be defined and measured in the mainstream of OC research work.

However, observing a well-known related body of knowledge on loyalty reveals a different picture, and I mean the research work around Albert Hirschman's famous model's *Exit, Voice and Loyalty*. This is the title of his book from 1970, and it was elaborated later by Rusbult *et al.* (1983, 1988), Withey and Cooper (1989) and Wehling and Scholl (1993). The model defines a range of behavioral modes of response in the face of organizational deterioration, or when organizations disregard the needs of their workforce.

1. Exit (active negative commitment);
2. Voice (active positive commitment by participation);
3. Loyalty (passive positive commitment);
4. Fence-sitting or silence — hesitating about the feeling of commitment and passive neutral commitment (added by Wehling and Scholl, 1993);
5. Neglect (passive negative commitment) — staying with indifference to the organization's problems and its future (added by Rusbult *et al.*, 1988).

These categories of OC have two advantages over previous concepts: they deal with actual behavior, and they do not hold any *a priori* assumption about psychological states, goals, values or culture of organizations. Individual employees may choose one or more behavioral modes of the above forms of commitment for a variety of reasons, including moral, calculative or affective causes. Hirschman himself was preoccupied with the economic nature of Exit and the political character of Voice, namely, the fight for a change in the system. Other researchers studied the psychological and social characteristics of Loyalty, Neglect and Fence-sitting (Lachman and Noy, 1996; Turnley and Feldman, 1999; Wehling and Scholl, 1993). Of course, choosing Exit, Voice or Loyalty may be related to a variety of reasons, including affective, continuance and normative blend of motives. However, this model is rarely referred to in the mainstream research literature on OC, though, except for Hirschman himself, who was an economist, all other researchers in the field are coming from organizational behavior and related disciplines. One of these rare occasions is the study of Davis-Blake *et al.* (2003), who examined how the structure of the workforce affects exit, voice and loyalty among standard employees (with permanent employment directly with the employer) and non-standard employees (with agency-temporary employment) in the same jobs. They found, beyond some other contingencies, that workforce blending decreased standard employees' loyalty, and increased their interest both in leaving their organizations and in exercising voice through unionization. However, as a rule, defining commitment as an active or passive loyalty behavior under unrewarding circumstances, is almost non-existent in the OC literature, and, curiously enough, the term "Loyalty" is rare in the OC discourse.

Chapter 3

Measuring Organizational Commitment

Among several research tools, two instruments are at the core of empirical research on organizational commitment (OC). One is the Organizational Commitment Questionnaire (OCQ) that was developed by Mowday *et al.* (1979). The second tool is the three-dimensional OC, developed by Allen and Meyer (1990).

A 15-item OCQ was developed by Porter *et al.* (1974) and codified by Mowday *et al.* (1979). They interviewed 2,563 employees in nine widely diverse work organizations over a nine-year period. Job classifications of those interviewed included public employees, classified university employees, hospital personnel, bank and telephone company employees, scientists and engineers, auto company managers, psychiatric technicians and retail management trainees. Cook and Wall interviewed 650 United Kingdom blue-collar workers in two separate studies. The samples were composed of full-time skilled, semi-skilled and unskilled male workers in manufacturing industries.

Cook and Wall (1980) developed a shorter nine-item version scale, adapted from the longer OCQ, designed for a working-class population. It was supposed to capture three of the following interrelated dimensions: (a) acceptance of the organization's values (identification), (b) willingness to exert effort on behalf of the organization (involvement) and (c) a desire to remain an employee of the organization (loyalty).

The following items make up the Cook and Wall's questionnaire of OC. Responses are on a seven-point range (*R* is for reversal items) as given in the following:

1. I am quite proud to be able to tell people who it is I work for.
2. I sometimes feel like leaving this employment for good (*R*).
3. I am not willing to put myself out just to help the organization (*R*).
4. Even if the firm were not doing too well financially, I would be reluctant to change to another employer.
5. I feel myself to be part of the organization.
6. In my work I like to feel I am making some effort, not just for myself but for the organization as well.
7. The offer of a bit more money with another employer would not seriously make me think of changing my job.
8. I would not recommend a close friend to join our staff (*R*).
9. To know that my own work had made a contribution to the good of the organization would please me.

Cook and Wall reported convergent reliability (Cronbach's α) of 0.87 and 0.80 for their two samples. However, Mowday *et al.* and Cook and Wall failed to validate the theoretically three-derived dimensions. Mowday *et al.*'s factor analysis of the 15-item OCQ revealed only a single factor solution. Also, Price and Mueller (1986, p. 77) reported that there is no empirical support for claiming that the items of the Cook and Wall scale differentiate three distinct dimensions of commitment. Morrow (1983), using facet design to compare and contrast related concepts, disclosed a redundancy among different foci of commitment. She showed, for example, that the identification component of the Mowday–Cook–Wall scales subsumes measures of job involvement. Price and Mueller (1986, p. 81) also noted an ambiguity between Mowday *et al.*'s distinction between commitment and satisfaction.

Angle and Perry (1981) found similar results. A factor analysis of the 15-item Porter OCQ revealed almost identical characteristics between two dimensions or subscales: a value commitment, comprising items of identification and involvement, and items indicating a commitment to retain membership in the organization. Bar-Haim and Berman (1992) researched the dimensionality of OC scale of Cook and Wall among 1,299 employees in 14 major Israeli industrial enterprises, representing a wide range of products produced, technology, size of organization and type of community where the organizations were located, over a three-year period (1984 to 1986). Using a factor analysis, the nine items of Cook and Wall's scale yielded two different measures of OC: identification on the first factor and loyalty on the second factor. They interpreted this as a distinction between passive and active OC, hidden in the original scales, that could prove useful in understanding the behavior of different populations of industrial workers.

Nowadays, the most accepted tool to measure OC is that of Alan and Meyer (1990). This questionnaire is composed, in its full length, of 24 items, eight items in each of the following claimed dimension: affective commitment scale (ACS), continuance commitment scale (CCS) and normative commitment scale (NCS). It also has a shortened version with six items per dimension:

- *Affective Commitment Scale Items*:

  1. I would be very happy to spend the rest of my career in this organization.
  2. I really feel as if this organization's problems are my own.
  3. I do not feel like "part of my family" at this organization (*R*).
  4. I do not feel "emotionally attached" to this organization (*R*).
  5. This organization has a great deal of personal meaning for me.
  6. I do not feel a strong sense of belonging to this organization (*R*).

- *Continuance Commitment Scale Items*:

  7. It would be very hard for me to leave my job at this organization right now even if I wanted to.
  8. Too much of my life would be disrupted if I leave my organization.
  9. Right now, staying with my job at this organization is a matter of necessity as much as desire.
  10. I believe I have too few options to consider leaving this organization.
  11. One of the few negative consequences of leaving my job at this organization would be the scarcity of available alternatives elsewhere.

12. One of the major reasons I continue to work for this organization is that leaving would require considerable personal sacrifice.

- *Normative Commitment Scale Items*:

13. I do not feel any obligation to remain with my organization (*R*).
14. Even if it were to my advantage, I do not feel it would be right to leave.
15. I would feel guilty if I left this organization now.
16. This organization deserves my loyalty.
17. I would not leave my organization right now because of my sense of obligation to it.
18. I owe a great deal to this organization.

Since the intensive preoccupation with the methodology of OC research in the nineties, the three-dimensional questionnaire of Allen and Meyer has become canonical. Today, validation of this questionnaire is not frequent and is performed mainly to check for cultural biases. Such is the study of Abdullah (2011) in the Pakistani context (found reliable), or of Karim and Noor (2006) in the Malaysian context (found reliable, but only ACS and CCS were examined, and among Malaysian academic librarians).

The Values' Base of OC as a Methodological Problem

We saw that social values' base of OC is a consistent element in almost any theory of OC. Why is this so? The place of values in organizational behavior stems from several theoretical points of view. One of the most accepted frameworks is the concept of congruence between characteristics of the individual and characteristics of the organization as a predictor of organizational attitudes and behavior (Chatman, 1989; Edwards, 1994). Kristof (1996) defined such a person–organization fit as "the compatibility between people and organizations that occurs when: (a) at least one entity provides what the other needs, or (b) they share similar fundamental characteristics, or (c) both" (p. 5).

Values are characteristics that both employees and organizations may share. One can easily show that employees would be more comfortable in a workplace that is consistent with their values. Imagine an individual who values "honesty", who is working in an organization that emphasizes "getting the job done at all costs". In all likelihood, the result of placing people in situations at odds with their personal values will not be positive for either the employees or the organization. Not only could employees' well-being be at risk, but it is also possible that they would be less devoted to the organization and possibly less productive.

Rokeach (1973, p. 5) in a seminal work defined a value as "an enduring belief that a specific mode of conduct or end-state of existence is personally or socially preferable to an opposite or converse mode of control". In a similar way, Dose (1997, pp. 227–228) defines values as "evaluative standards relating to work or the work environment by which individuals discern what is "right" or assess the importance of preferences". McDonald and Gandz (1991), Seligman and Katz (1996), Meyer *et al.* (1993) and others modified Rokeach's original list for use in the organizational context.[1] Finegan (2000) applied the 24-item questionnaire of McDonald (1993) in her study, and showed its consistency with the value dimensions distinguished by Schwartz and Bilsky (1987).

In this book, the value dimension in the context of OC is approached in a different way. Since the focus of this study is OC, and since one of the major bases of commitment is norms and values, I need to control for the general propensity of employees to adhere to any set of values when they refer to the normative dimension OC. Thus, the dimensionality or factor structure of a set of values is less relevant here, and only the overall score of the importance of any set of values is counted.[2]

---

[1] Rokeach's scale is based on rank-order values, which results in statistical problems (Edwards, 1994). In the McDonald and Gandz's revised version, the values are rated rather than rank-ordered.

[2] However, I could not avoid the curiosity about the factor structure of the values set in my study (see later). Therefore, I applied the same factor analysis as Finegan did and more (I explored three, four and the maximum five factor solutions that I had in my data), and I also applied a non-metric Guttman–Lingoes smallest space analysis (SSA), but failed to reconstruct her four-factor structure of values.

Organizational Citizenship Behavior (OCB) as a Measure of Commitment

A note should be added at this point about a related concept and measure of commitment, namely, OCB. In a study on OCB, Schappe (1998) found that only OC predicts OCB (the other unsupported predictors were job satisfaction and fairness perceptions, and all the three variables were related to OCB in a meta-analysis on 55 studies by Organ and Ryan (1995)).

Numerous studies define OCB as a category of extra-role behavior, or in Organ's (1988, p. 4) words: "individual behavior that is discretionary, not directly or explicitly recognized by the formal reward system, and that in the aggregate promotes the effective functioning of the organization". No doubt, OC is an extra-role behavior as well. However, at the moment, OCB scales suffer from similar problems of the old OC scales. For example, Williams and Anderson (1991) argue that there is a conceptual overlap between job satisfaction and OC, and the significant relationships that have been found using only job satisfaction or OC to predict OCB are potentially spurious.[3] It also lacks the unique property of OC as a pure behavior of choice when the organization is at crossroads.

In a rare study on the relationships among OC, job satisfaction, procedural justice and OCB, Schappe (1998) showed that, contrary to findings from previous research, when considering job satisfaction, procedural justice perceptions and OC as predictors, only OC emerged as a significant predictor of OCB.

Weiner (1972), Scholl (1981) and Kanter (1972) have already discussed this. Scholl suggested that because commitment maintains behavioral direction when there is little expectation of formal organizational rewards for performance, it is a likely determinant of OCB. Weiner suggested that commitment is responsible for behaviors that do not depend primarily on reinforcements or punishment. Rosabeth Kanter, in her

---

[3] The often-cited five dimensions of OCB, namely, altruism, conscientiousness, courtesy, sportsmanship and civic virtue, are rarely fully used in concrete research works or in standard forms. So, there is a significant gap between this extra-role category and its measurement.

seminal work, conceptualized commitment as a central concern of the American communes in the 19th century, precisely because it was so difficult for the members to comply with their demanding way of life.

Therefore, OCB is a litmus test for OC. As Schappe said, following Organ (1988), OCBs are not mandated by job descriptions, they are rarely linked directly to the job or, more specifically, to job performance.

OCB exists outside of the domain of traditional behavior that "gets the job done", yet citizenship behavior is still an important element of an employee's overall contribution to an organization. This remark is appropriate for OC as well. Employees may engage in behaviors that are beneficial to co-workers, superiors or the organization as a whole. Thus, the managers' ability to motivate employees by relying on formal reward structures to reinforce specific role requirements is limited.

The weakness of the assertion that OC is a part of reward system in the workplace is evident in some studies. For example, Boroff and Lewin (1997) developed a model of employee voice and employee intent to exit the firm. They found that loyal employees who experienced unfair workplace treatment primarily responded by suffering in silence.

Chapter 4

Some Research Evidence on Organizational Commitment in its Golden Age

As noted above, empirical research on organizational commitment (OC) dates back to the fifties. The works of Becker (1960), Kelman (1958), Etzioni (1961), Kanter (1968) and Saunders (1956) are among the oldest studies that were focused on commitment in the context of organizational behavior. The focus of these studies is on the forms and mechanisms of attachment to organizations (in the case of Kanter's study, the commitment to communes).

In the "golden age" of the research on OC, many studies were focused primarily on the effect of OC on employee turnover and intentions to leave (Cohen, 1993; Ingersoll et al., 2000; Mowday et al., 1979; Reilly and Orsak; Rusbult and Fan-nell, 1983). In a meta-analysis study, Cohen (1993) analyzed the correlation between OC and turnover rate among 36 samples in studies between 1967 and 1991. In justifying the cause of the research, he relied on Mowday et al. (1979) and remarked that "Most attention given to the concept of OC results from its relationship with turnover. By definition, highly committed employees wish to remain with their employing organizations. So, if turnover is the problem, OC is the solution." (p. 1140)

In a comprehensive study, Burton *et al.* (2002) survey the developments of empirical studies in the field of OC, from research that was focused on an individual's emotional attachment to an organization (Mowday *et al.*, 1979), through the meta-analysis by Farrell and Stamm (1988) on the OC's negative relationship with absence ($r = -0.23$), to the more comprehensive view of Meyer and Allen (1990, 1997). A variety of studies have examined the relationship between the different types of commitment and absenteeism. Overall, it appears that affective commitment has the strongest relation with absence behavior (Meyer and Allen, 1997). The results for normative commitment are less consistent. Meyer *et al.* (1993) found that normative commitment was negatively related to absenteeism while Somers (1995) found no relationship between normative commitment and absenteeism.[1] Finally, continuance commitment has not found strong support in the absenteeism literature (e.g., Mayer and Schoorman, 1992). Burton *et al.* (2002) also remind us that the majority of these studies have been conducted on nurses in large hospitals.

Due to the weak effect of the various dimensions of OC on absenteeism, Meyer and Allen (1997) and Johns (1997) have suggested to see if these attitudes affect absenteeism indirectly. Rhodes and Steers (1990) explored motivation to attend as one possible intervening variable. It was expected that affective and normative commitment will be strongly related to a person's motivation to attend, while continuance commitment will have a lesser impact. It could be expected that if employees have high levels of affective commitment toward their working organization, they would be more likely to be motivated to attend work every day. Or, if employees feel they ought to go to work each day (normative commitment), this should be strongly related to motivation to attend. On the other hand, if employees feel they have to go to work (continuance commitment), a weaker relationship with motivation to attend could be expected.

However, the most conspicuous observation in retrospect is the definition of employee turnover, which in fact is employee leaving as an outcome of poor OC, whereas, it is a behavior of the commitment itself albeit a negative one. It is a rare instant in organizational behavior that you

---

[1] Meyer *et al.* (1993) used a self-reported measure of absences while Somers (1995) used organizational records to measure the total number of days absent per employee.

can observe pure behavior and not indirect manifestations of it in forms of attitudes, intentions and scholarly guesses about the content of the black box. Ontologically, it is less obvious to observe staying in the organization (positive commitment) because it is not an unambiguous active form of commitment. Employees who are present in their jobs in their employing organizations are not necessarily committed to their organizations. They might be, but mere presence is not a sufficient condition. Leavers (those who made turnover), however, may have all the proper psychological states ("bases" in OC jargon) to fit the title of committed employees, but they lost the behavioral ticket to this club, because they are not there.[2]

Other studies at that time occupy a good deal with job satisfaction. This attitudinal behavior has been always predominant in this area. Spector (1996) found that over 12,400 published research studies focused on job satisfaction. Job satisfaction was found to be correlated with performance, pay, turnover, absenteeism, health and stress, life satisfaction, education, gender, race and age, to name some of the more common correlates. Keller (1997) found correlations with job involvement and OC as well, and Meyer *et al.* (1993) found that their scales were related strongly to job satisfaction, emotional attachment and financial need. Similar findings were produced by Irving *et al.* (1997). On the other hand, no sufficient evidence was accumulated to show that employees with high OC are more productive (Schrader, 2010).

---

[2] *Full disclosure*: For me, the most convincing examples were my mother and her cousin, who emigrated in the thirties of the 20th century from Europe. She went to Israel and joined a *Kibbutz* (a collective commune), where I was born. She was a dedicated hard worker, "committed" in Rosabeth Kantor's terms, *and hated* this way of life. Her cousin went to Brazil and became a rich man. He was an enthusiast for the ideas and practices of the *Kibbutz*. According to the mainstream OC studies, my mother was alienated and uncommitted, while her cousin was highly committed to the *Kibbutz* by both affective and normative dimensions. However, my mother lived 60 years in a *Kibbutz*, and her cousin lived the same period as a wealthy capitalist in Brazil.

Chapter 5

Organizational Commitment as a Case of Scientific Disarray

Empirical findings on organizational commitment (OC) do not always confirm teaching and organizational development (OD) practices. Thus, in a standard textbook on organizational behavior in the eighties of the 20th century (Baron and Greenberg, 1986, p. 164), we find the following statement: "Organizational commitment appears to exert powerful effects on several aspects of work behavior." The effects are summarized as follows:

- *Factors tending to increase OC:*

  1. Motivating potential of specific job
  2. High level of responsibility
  3. High level of autonomy
  4. Satisfaction with own level of work performance
  5. Seniority/tenure
  6. High quality of supervision
  7. Fair appraisals

- *Factors tending to reduce OC:*

  1. Role ambiguity
  2. Job tension

3. Availability of other employment opportunities
4. Belief that company does not care about employees
5. Use of punishment by supervisors

No convincing empirical evidence is presented to support these lists. However, they typically represent expectation from OC to be a sort of a heavy-duty motivational engine in the workplace.

However, work motivation was not on the agenda of the golden age research on OC and was hardly mentioned. The research products were good enough to establish the construct of OC as an independent field of inquiry. Only in the last decade or so, there are research efforts to merge the OC body of knowledge with the research corpus of work motivation and to show that OC is a type of a motivation engine (Meyer *et al.*, 2004). This intellectual endeavor to create a new research agenda with the aim of merging OC with work motivation, apparently, is a natural scientific development, where two matured fields are ripe for integration. However, unfortunately, I see this project as an intellectual *cul-de-sac*. The attempts of Meyer, whose studies on OC are perhaps the most comprehensive in the field, to study OC in the framework of work motivation theory are surprising. This is because there are scarcely research works that link between OC and work motivation. Looking, for example, in the research database PROQUEST, reveals that until June 2016, there were 735 scholarly full-text titles over several decades, which included the term ORGANIZATIONAL COMMITMENT. However, there were merely eight (!) scholarly full-text cited items, which included ORGANIZATIONAL COMMITMENT **AND** WORK MOTIVATION in their titles. These few studies include five articles, which have ORGANIZATIONAL COMMITMENT **AND** MOTIVATION in their titles, and only three (!) articles, which include ORGANIZATIONAL COMMITMENT **AND** WORK MOTIVATION in their titles.

To check again this amazing finding, I went also to the research database EBSCO, which is less oriented toward organizational behavior and management science, and more toward the social sciences in general. The state of affairs is not better: on June 2016, there were 213 peer reviewed full-text articles with ORGANIZATIONAL COMMITMENT in the titles. However, only one (!) article found with the title ORGANIZATIONAL

COMMITMENT **AND** MOTIVATION, and none (!) with the title ORGANIZATIONAL COMMITMENT **AND** WORK MOTIVATION. Thus, the attempt to jump on the motivation carriage after several decades of ignoring motivation by OC research community, either as an antecedent, intervening or as an outcome, is astounding. In the light of the efforts here to revise the conceptualization of OC, it seems that the attempts to join up the work motivation research corpus are a rear battle of the old paradigm of OC that has been exhausted.

Both the *raison d'etre* and research interest in OC in Western countries are declining. Central researchers in the field, recognizing this decline on the side of employers, suggest changing the foci of commitment: if not the organization, turn to work and team groups, the job itself, the supervisor, the career and so forth — there is enough room to express useful affective, continuance and normative attitudes toward new objects. However, since these alternative foci are occupied by other strong organizational behavior and social psychology theories, the chance for a renaissance is perhaps not promising.

The main axis of the integration project is to consider commitment behavior as a discretionary area of beyond work duties, and the secondary axis is to move from OC to other foci of commitment, and hope that this shift is still beneficial to managers and employees (albeit, unfortunately, not directly to the organization).

Adhering to extra-role (discretionary) behavior is perhaps not very much promising, because managers and many researchers are nowadays more interested in the twin phenomenon of organizational citizenship behavior (OCB). The problem is not with reliability or validity of the current OC construct. Affective and normative commitments do predict some organizational behavior outcomes (continuance OC is less predictive). However, their added value for understanding work motivation is not substantial, despite of managerial rhetoric in the field. Employers do not mind to name hard work, high performance, devotion and loyalty by commitment, extreme motivation or whatever. As a matter of fact, they do not see the semantic differences. Researchers, on the other hand, do not see a dramatic statistical added value to the explained variance in work motivation outcomes.

The problem of the concept OC is in its basic assumptions, in particular, the assumption that commitment is a motivational force. The second wrong assumption is that, as a motivational force, it entails a potential for greater rewards, because it is a promise for greater work investment, endurance and persistence over longer time.

The taken-for-granted assumption about the transactional character of commitment is obvious in all the major texts in the field. Morrow (1993, p. xvii) opens her book saying that "A lack of commitment or loyalty has been cited as an explanation for employee absenteeism, turnover, reduced effort expenditure, theft, job dissatisfaction and unwillingness to be relocated…". All the imminent scholars in the field suggest various explanations for this lack of or diminishing commitment with a common denominator — a breach of the unwritten, but taken-for-granted psychological contract or a transaction between employees and employers to supply commitment in return for all or some of the above employment conditions.

Another version of the transactional approach to commitment is that of Lincoln and Kalleberg (1990). They conceptualize commitment as a control structure to tie employees to their employing organization (commitment-maximizing) and explore the "commitment gap" between American corporations and Japanese welfare corporations. They assume that low commitment among employees in American workplaces is dangerous to the survival and viability of these organizations in comparison with the highly committed employees in the welfare corporatism regime and culture of Japanese organizations.

The demand for commitment in organizations is a demand to pay off an obligation to stay, support and undertaking responsibilities in case of difficulties, dangers and threats. However, the reason for commitment in organizations is not enhancing motivation or performance. This can be done in many ways by extrinsic and intrinsic rewards, or by developing convincing focus of identification and attachment.

As with life insurance, people do not hope for the case that their insurance will be paid off, so organizations should not strive to materialize their employees' commitment. Because when they need it, they are in trouble, they cannot reward properly, the foci of identification and attachment are weak and they are dependent on the goodwill of their employees, suppliers and creditors.

However, this is not the state of the art of OC in the research literature. Zangaro (2001), among the few who bothered to check the dictionary, hastens to add (after Porter *et al.*, 1974, p. 14) that "… a person who is committed to an organization should then be dedicated and have a strong belief in the organization's goals and values." And I ask WHY? "Pledging to fulfill an obligation to someone or something" is one thing, but "to have a strong belief in organization's goals and values" is quite a different thing, and is neither logically nor empirically, a necessary condition to commitment.

In everyday life, we make commitments because we cannot achieve our goals or wishes without pledging obligations — we do it when we need money from the bank or friends; we buy an insurance policy, with the hope that we never realize the obligations in these policies; we make future promises to our children and request them to keep promises and we undertake vows to our spouse. Apparently, we do not need these promises, because we have genuine feelings and authentic statements of love and we reciprocate and share everything. However, we may need commitment as an act of fulfilling promises in the future if and when relationships change. So, commitment is reserved for undesired situations.

In most cases, obligations, debts and other forms of commitment are not pleasant or welcome. We are not motivated by commitment, and commitment does not arouse satisfaction. But commitment is required to guarantee fulfillment of obligations. Is OC different from this straightforward meaning?

The only world where commitment has elevated to the status of a desired state is the world of work and work organizations. Only there we hear and read again and again that managers are supposed to develop OC among their employees, and that good workers are those who are high performers with full of satisfaction, motivation AND commitment to their employing organization. Oh well, satisfaction–motivation–performance! That may or may not hold; the mountain of research studies about this trinity is not conclusive yet. But why to add OC to this *Cholent*? (Jewish meat stew traditionally eaten on the *Sabbath*). Why the treatment of commitment in organized settings is so different from the use of it in the rest of the world? Why commitment is supposed to act as a medicine to productivity problems and other behavioral diseases in the workplace, such as turnover, lateness, absenteeism, low morale and other symptoms of escapism and poor organizational citizenship?

My argument is that by subjugating commitment to another form of motivated and rewarded behaviors, scientists and practitioners (mostly managers) miss the real meaning and power of commitment. When employers and managers recognize OC as another instrument in the motivating toolbox and signal it to their employees, they waste their time. Employees learn very quickly to include this signal in their balance of rewards and contributions, and not as a unique consideration in their decision to stay or leave. To put it directly, the derived advice to employers is to motivate their employees and cause them to like their workplace, but, hopefully, never use commitment for that.

Employers cannot guarantee their employees' commitment, but only hope for it, when worse comes to worst. This is the real meaning of commitment in other spheres of life, as are reflected, for example, in the wedding vows and marriage contracts. Namely, commitment is not needed in times of love and reciprocity. Commitment is needed only when other mechanisms of exchange and reciprocity do not function properly. However, this meaning of OC is rarely found in the research on OC.

The reasons for this mistreatment are built-in the historical development of the research field of OC. However, it is also built in every organization that is programmed to control the scarcest resource of employees' willingness to stay and contribute to their employing organization. Therefore, OC is sought in any blend of emotional, moral and instrumental ingredients. But commitment, first and foremost, is about fulfilling obligations. Overlooking this dimension of commitment biases the research and application of OC.

The failure to account for the obligation dimension is evident in most studies on OC that use attitude surveys to measure it. Telling a researcher that you are happy with your pay or your boss and therefore you will recommend a friend to join the organization, and since you admire your firm and feel total agreement with its goals and values, you never be late or absent from work, are perhaps valid signs of organizational identification or work motivation, but not necessarily indications of commitment.

This is because commitment is not a state of mind, but a behavioral act of fulfilling an obligation or a promise to fulfill it. It may relate to the current employee's satisfaction or performance, and an employer may request his employees to fulfill an unpleasant, burdensome obligations in the future, but the willingness to obligate beyond the labor and psychological contract and beyond the agreed reward system (which already contains various levels of expectations for doing things beyond duty) is quite a different story.

In organizational context, concrete commitment is expressed in staying, supporting or undertaking and carrying the burden. However, these behaviors of commitment do not coincide with the definitions of Meyer and Allen (1997), who dominate the recent research on OC. They abbreviate their multi-dimensional conception of OC to three questions: "want to stay?" for affective commitment, "have to stay?" for continuance commitment and "ought to stay?" for normative commitment (*ibid*, p. 93).

For employees who **want to stay**, there is no problem of commitment, they want it anyway, because they like their organization and proud of it and there is no obligation or pledging in staying and contributing to it. For those who **have to stay**, leaving is not an option or too costly, because they may lose accumulated occupational and organizational assets and investments in skills, pension rights, fringe benefits, status, friends and so forth. Thus, while staying is a rational and self-interested behavior for continuance reasons, commitment is about voluntary staying, supporting and undertaking responsibilities against one's best interests, with high chance of **losing** assets. Therefore, this is not commitment but compliance in the absence of alternatives.

So, only the **"ought to stay"** component remains a true base of commitment, provided that employees ought to fulfill obligations. But normative obligation has a double meaning. On the one hand, fulfilling obligations is a normal and expected behavior everywhere, including organizations. Usually, employees who accept the terms of their formal and informal employment contract, do what they are told to do **with or without** consent, motivation, enthusiasm, identification and beliefs. Question is how much employing organizations can manipulate the level of normative commitment **without** persuasion, bargaining, rewards, or quality of work life, and how much this is a taken-for-granted side of commitment behavior in organizations.

On the other hand, normative behavior is also about obligations that employees **do not have to fulfill** but chose to do so. Perhaps, this is the praised behavior, but fulfilling obligations is almost absent in the main stream of OC research, and the non-instrumental commitment is defined only in terms of loyalty, identification, internalization of organizational goals and emotional attachment. Though, normative obligations are suggested as partial explanation for this non-instrumental behavior, what is missing is unrewarded work behavior beyond duty in "normal" times, and in times of deep organizational crisis, when employers cannot reciprocate their committed employees. So, how much of "ought to stay" is relevant when one side ceases to give in return anything to the other side, the workforce.

The idiosyncratic use of the concept commitment in organizational behavior is even more embarrassing when we check its use in neighboring fields, such as industrial and behavioral economics. For example, there is extensive research literature on exchange theory in transaction relationships, where commitment conforms to the standard lingual meaning. The weakness of the assertion that OC is a part of exchange system in the workplace is evident in many studies. For example, Boroff and Lewin (1997) developed a model of employee voice and employee intent to exit the firm. They found that loyal employees who experienced unfair workplace treatment primarily responded by suffering in silence.

The disarray in the conceptualization of OC steams from three sources: the confusion between commitment and psychological attachment and bonding states, the confusion between attitudes and behavior and the intellectual eagerness of some academic leaders in the field of organizational behavior "to help" organizations to reduce turnover rates and other "negative" employees' behaviors. All these sources are documents in many studies on OC and statements by eminent scholars in the field.

As discussed in the earlier chapters, the strongest practical motive to explore and use OC was to reduce turnover rates in era of full employment, stable labor relations and steady economic growth. This was also the era of a revolution of rising expectations of the young generation of employees of that time, who wanted self-fulfillment at work, not "only" the first four layers of Maslow's hierarchy of needs. So, harnessing research knowledge in the service of the nation's productive forces, namely, employing organizations and employees, appeared both scientifically and morally challenging and important. The other sources of this disarray are connected to epistemological issues in behavioral and management sciences — the inability to crack the black box of organizational behaviors and the scientific socialization of researchers in the field.

Ironically, **continuance,** which according to most of the researched knowledge, has no significant relations with measures of organizational performance, and inverse relations with withdrawal behavior, is most relevant to the revised concept that is suggested here, namely, obligatory or constrained behavior in the absence of occupational and organizational alternatives. Of course, this is not a very welcome behavior from points of view of work motivation theory or human resource management (HRM).

Chapter 6

The Escape from Organizational Commitment by Employing Organizations

Until a couple of decades ago, employers made great efforts to foster organizational commitment (OC) among their employees in order to secure the stay and continuance of employees' contributions in the face of high demand for labor, work alienation and temptations to exit and move to other employers. Thus, it is not surprising that many studies were focused on the effect of transactional OC on employee turnover (Gardner, 1992; Cohen, 1993; Ingersoll *et al.*, 2000; Mowday *et al.*, 1979; Reilly and Orsak, 1991).

However, there are numerous indications that the taken-for-granted assumption that OC is good for employers as well as for employees has been eroding. The recent decades of advanced technology and globalization have witnessed major changes in the world of work, in the direction of downsizing, outsourcing labor activities and restructuring organizations into leaner entities, which systematically strive to avoid long-term commitment to their workforce. Even older and well-established organizations, which continue to employ a large core of their own workforce, have resorted to the use of what are variously termed atypical, non-standard, flexible jobs (which generally mean part-time work, temporary employment, including agency employment).

The need to re-examine the meaning and relevance of OC is not new. Baruch (1998), in a polemical paper, and Mowday (2003), one of the founders of the field, in candid statements, raised the question of OC relevancy today. Baruch referred to business changes, and the weakening of the assertion that OC leads to a set of desired outputs in times of mutual commitment between organizations and their employees. He described (in the end of the nineties of the 20th century) the new era of human resource management and industrial relation systems, characterized by frequent redundancies and downsizing processes, and low commitment from organizations to their employees, which was followed by a reduced level of OC. His stance is pragmatic: OC requires trust and mutuality in relationships. These preconditions are not sustained in the new world of work, and therefore OC lost its *raison d'etre*.

Chapter 7

Organizational Commitment: A Redefinition

The justification to redefine the concept of organizational commitment (OC) in this book is twofold: the change in the current world of work, which is experiencing an escape from commitment, and secondly, the epistemological argument that the current concept of OC misses the facet of unrewarded forms of commitment behavior.

The emergence of globalized, technology-driven world of work has a fundamental effect on the bonds between employees and their employing organizations. The managerial efforts to secure retention, quality of working life and satisfaction at work have been replaced by eliminating permanent employment and secure income from work. Instead, workforce of low-paid, low-security jobs, non-unionized, temporary work, contract employment and other atypical work arrangements have emerged. The needs of employers have profoundly changed. Their concerns are about flexibility, not commitment. *They do not need OC anymore.* However, in the mainstream research on OC, the assumption that OC is mutually good for employees and employers still prevails.

Nevertheless, even disregarding the new reality in the world of work, the scientific concept of OC itself has a serious problem of validity. In everyday life, we make commitments and pledge obligations — we do it when we borrow money from the bank or from friends or when we undertake vows to our spouse. Apparently, we do not need these promises; when there is trust, we have genuine feelings of love. However, we may need commitment to guarantee the fulfillment of the promised obligations in the future, when relationships and circumstances change. Therefore, obligations, debts and other forms of commitment are neither pleasant nor welcome: we are not motivated by commitment, and commitment does not arouse our satisfaction. This argument applies to OC as well.

However, this aspect of fulfilling obligations is completely absent from the current definition of OC. We have "bases" or motives for OC, but not manifest or visible behaviors of fulfilling duties and obligations. When we pay the monthly bill of mortgage, we show a commitment to our debt. When we stay and treat our helpless old parents, we reveal our commitment to them. When a worker stays and continues doing his job despite his employer's inability to pay him, it is a manifestation of OC. Just expressing confident attitudes of emotional feelings or of desirable values toward the employing organization is not enough and does not encompass the essence of commitment.

Another major *lacuna* in the current definition of OC is its lack of distinction from related concepts, such as work motivation or work satisfaction. Empirically, items of OC questionnaires are often similar to items in the tools to measure motivation and satisfaction. However, beyond measurement similarity, OC's tools were developed to capture similar phenomena, namely, procedures that attach employees to their workplace and work and drive them to make efforts on behalf of their employers. However, without specified distinctiveness between OC and other similar organizational behaviors, its strength as a unique phenomenon is questionable.

What make OC unique are two characteristics: its behavioral facet and the availability of alternatives to its carriers, namely, committed employees.

A New Mapping Sentence for OC

In this redefinition technique, another two elements are added to the three bases of OC (emotional, normative and utilitarian), as described in the following mapping sentence:

This mapping sentence is read as follows:

- OC is displayed by making extra efforts on behalf of the employing organization (Behavioral OC – **BOC**), and/or performing unrewarded

Figure 7.1. New Semantic Space of OC (Facets R and F are New)

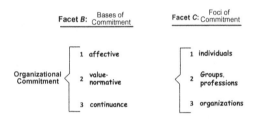

Figure 7.2. Old Semantic Space of Organization Commitment

and unpleasant routine duties (**unrewarded BOC**) and/or *unrewarded shouldering* of duties in troubled time to save the employing organization (**extreme Sisyphean unrewarded BOC**, which lacks any of the above three motivational bases.

- BOC is enabled **with or without** emotional, normative and utilitarian motives **only** for employees with occupational alternatives and/or organizational resources.

- So, according to the new redefinition, it is a unique behavior of unrewarded employees with alternatives in the labor market or in their workplace, who stay despite their ability to leave for a more secure and rewarding workplace.

We can see that according to this definition only facet F_1 postulates general extra efforts on behalf of the employing organization, which may indicate work motivation and other bases of OC. All other states are confined to unrewarded behavior of employees in the workplace. This is because only in these states, the revised OC has an added value to our understanding of the field. Since, there is no reason to stay or commit to anything in the workplace nowadays beyond duty, this is the only behavior of delivery, carried out under the worst conditions, when the employing organization is unable or unwilling to reward it.

Most of the research on OC is about Facet B. The new mapping sentence adds F_2 and F_3 as a range of unrewarded or underrewarded behaviors of commitment, from performing difficult/unpleasant/stressful/boring duties, which are not part of the employment contract, up to shouldering the burden to save the organization for no rewards or promises for rewards. The extreme (Sisyphean) version of unrewarded behavior of commitment is even without any apparent base (neither utilitarian nor affective or normative).

Another new facet in the definition of OC is the resources of the committed person (Facet R), which is required to control for factors that may limit free choice and voluntarism of the committed person. These resources are in two groups: occupational and income alternatives that employees may have if they want to leave their workplace, and organizational status and support assets in their workplace. These resources considerably affect their degrees of freedom in any commitment behavior or decision.

Let us look at Table 1. It displays **theoretical** profiles or combinations of OC events in the Cartesian space under the new mapping sentence. While each of the elements of the defined facets may have a continuous sequence, it has been reduced here to binary or dichotomous states to simplify the argument. Thus, we can see that the resources facet R has four profiles, composed of two binary states of occupational and income alternatives and organizational status and support; Facet B of OC bases has eight profiles of three binary states of affective, normative and instrumental bases; and the facet F of BOC forms has eight profiles of three binary states of rewarded BOC, unrewarded BOC and extreme unrewarded BOC.

However, not every theoretical profile is empirically expected. For example, BOC forms that are both rewarded and unrewarded are less expected, though, we may observe, in rare cases, mixed situations which are partly rewarded and partly unrewarded. Other profiles may be excluded because they do not conform to the new concept of OC. For example, a required condition for genuine OC is alternatives of employees

Table 1. Profiles of OC

Facet R: resources of committed persons	Facet B: OC bases	Facet F: forms of BOC
1 — Occupational and income alternatives	1 — Affective	1 — Making extra efforts on behalf of the employing organization *(Rewarded BOC)*
2 — Organizational status and support	2 — Normative	2 — Performing unrewarded and unpleasant routine duties *(Unrewarded BOC)*
	3 — Instrumental	3 — Unrewarded shouldering of duties to save the organization in trouble *(Extreme (Sisyphean) unrewarded BOC)*

Profiles BOC resources			Profiles of OC bases				Profiles of BOC forms			
#	1	2	#	1	2	3	#	1	2	3
A	–	–	a	–	–	–	a	–	–	–
B	+	–	b	+	–	–	b	+	–	–
C	+	+	c	+	+	–	c	+	+	–
D	–	+	d	+	+	+	d	+	+	+
			e	–	+	+	e	–	+	+
			f	–	–	+	f	–	–	+
			g	–	+	–	g	–	+	–
			h	+	–	+	h	+	–	+

in labor market or in the internal power system of the workplace *vis-à-vis* their employers. Thus, profile **a** of the resources facet *R*, which shows no alternatives at all, may be excluded.

The typical events or profiles of genuine OC are shadowed in Table 1. Accordingly, on facet *R* (resources), profiles **b**, **c** and **d** are possible combinations leading to real states of OC. Recall that true commitment in work organizations, according to the new definition, assumes the independence of the committed employee from the employer's resources and its organizational power. Without this resource autonomy, commitment may be rendered to the submissive loyalty of those who have no choice (for example, see profile R_a).

Among the profiles of facet **B** (bases of OC), profile B_a, which shows no apparent base of OC, is the only one that may explicate OC as unrewarded behavior. Other profiles of this facet are possible, but they "contaminate" the concept of OC with other explanations, such as work motivation or job security. Several studies show that profile B_b (mainly affective base of OC) often describes Western employees, while profile B_g (mainly normative base of BOC) is often typical of Japanese and Chinese employees. Watanabe and Takahashi (1999) show that the Japanese style of management strongly promotes employees' continuance commitment, rather than an affective one. Other studies also reveal weak affective base of commitment in Asian countries (Luthans *et al.*, 1985; Near, 1989; Tan and Akhtar, 1998; Keisuke, 2018).

On facet *F* (BOC forms), profiles F_e, F_f and F_g, which contain no rewarded BOC elements, are pure forms of unrewarded behavior regarding OC. Therefore, combinations of performing unrewarded and unpleasant routine duties (a light version of unrewarded BOC) AND unrewarded shouldering of duties to save the organization in trouble (extreme version of unrewarded BOC) illustrate this group of BOC forms. Other profiles of facet *F* represent mixed forms of rewarded and unrewarded behavioral forms, except for profile F_a, which is a case of no commitment at all. Recall that in the old definition of OC that relies solely on OC bases, this state is possible, with no actual commitment behavior.

Chapter 8

Empirical Study I of BOC: Voice as a Form of Behavioral Commitment

In Chapter 2, the EVL model is discussed as a neglected brick in the organizational commitment (OC) research. However, this brick is essential to the new approach presented here because it was, in my knowledge, the first attempt to display behavioral modes of commitment. In the well-known paradigm of Exit, Voice and Loyalty, suggested in 1970 by Albert Hirschman, Loyalty is barely elaborated. Hirschman himself concentrated on Exit as an economic means of coping with unsatisfied state, or Voice as a mode of political struggle to halt the system deterioration. Loyalty is treated as a residual category, reserved for those who have neither Exit alternatives nor will to fight for a change (Voice). It has been also indicated above that Hirschman's provocative EVL model is hardly cited or researched in organizational behavior in general and OC in particular. After an extensive review of the OC literature, including several careful literature surveys and meta-analyses (Mathiew and Zajac, 1990; Randall *et al.*, 1990), this surprising omission is confirmed.

The EVL model suggests several avenues to deal with discontent in organized systems in the face of two basic questions: (a) Are occupational or income alternatives available to members of the work community? (b) Are efforts made by members of the system to improve the work

Table 1.   Events of Potential True OC

Event	Occupational and income alternatives	Improvement efforts in face of discontent
1	Yes	No
2	No	Yes
3	Yes	Yes
4	No	No

organization in order to reduce discontent? Four states are displayed in Table 1, when answers are simplified to "yes" or "no" (not necessarily mutual exclusive).

Event 1 describes a system where employees have alternatives to their employment in the specific workplace. However, they do nothing to change or repair the system. Event 2 is the opposite case: employees have no alternatives, but attempt to improve the system. In event 3, employees do have alternatives to their discontented system, but they prefer to stay and make efforts to improve it. Event 4 displays a system where employees with neither alternatives nor attempts to change the situation.

According to EVL model, in events 1 and 4, where no efforts are made to improve the system, the organizational members are candidates for Exit. Event 2 is perhaps the case of Loyalty, namely, attempts to repair the system by employees who have no alternatives outside it. However, the most interesting event for our argument is 3. Here, employees, who have occupation and/or income alternatives outside the system, prefer to stay and attempt to repair it. Apparently, this is a case of unrewarded commitment behavior.

The lack of available Exit options and inaction regarding the improvement of the unsatisfied workplace (event 4) is perhaps the case of Neglect, which is not dealt in this study (see, Rusbult *et al.*, 1988; Rusbult *et al.*, 1986; Withey and Cooper, 1989).

The Study, Sample and Research Methods

In order to examine the relationships among employees' satisfaction, bases of OC and behavioral forms of OC, data from a research study on

EVL are reanalyzed (Bar-Hayim and Berman, 1992). Among 1,299 employees in 14 major Israeli industrial enterprises, representing a wide range of products, technology, size of enterprise and type of community where the enterprises were located, one-third of the employees in each enterprise were selected randomly for inclusion.

Satisfaction was measured by a reliable scale, made of Job Satisfaction, Pay satisfaction and Workplace Satisfaction. OC was measured by the Cook and Wall's (1980) nine-item scale, adapted from the longer Mowday *et al.*'s (1979) OCQ and designed for a working-class population. This commitment scale was measured in two ways: first, as a unidimensional additive scale of Identification with the organization, which defines an emotional attachment to the organization. Secondly, using a factor analysis, the nine items yielded two different measures of OC: Identification on the first factor and Loyalty to the organization on the second factor.[1]

Voice intention, which serves as a form of behavioral OC, was measured by the question: "Should employees give up part of their wages and salaries to prevent dismissal of other employees in your plant". 56% of the respondents were in agreement categories, 30% were in disagreement categories and 14% were in the neutral category. Exit intention, which indicates negative behavioral commitment, was measured by the "lottery question": suppose you would win enough money in a lottery to live comfortable all your life, would you: (1) stop working, (2) continue working but in a different workplace, (3) continue working in this place, but in a different job, (4) continue working in this place, same job, but part time, (5) continue working in this place, same job, full time. 54% chose the last option (full time, same job, same workplace), 8% answered that they would stop working and 38% chose the intermediate options.

In Figure 8.1, two EVL models are tested: basic and refined models.

In the basic EVL model, **Satisfaction** correlates directly and positively with OC as a state of identification and slightly with **Voice** as behavioral commitment. However, most of the **Satisfaction** effect on **Voice** is mediated by commitment as identification, which remains the prime predictor of **Voice** intentions. However, in the refined model, even

---

[1] The side-bets aspect of OC, which is the aggregate effect of investing life time in the work organization, was not well separated as a single factor (See Cohen and Lowenberg, 1990).

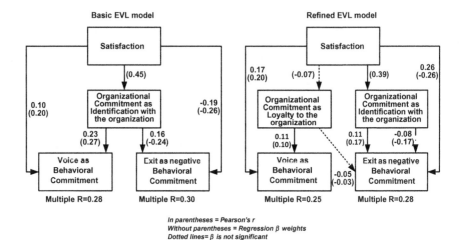

Figure 8.1. Relationships Among Employees' Satisfaction, Forms of OC and EVL (Behavioral OC)

this slight effect disappears and only **dissatisfaction** relates to **Exit** intentions (negative behavioral commitment). **Voice** intentions (positive behavioral commitment) are predicted mainly by non-behavioral commitment — either as an additive unidimensional overall measure of identification, or as two separate scales: Identification with the organization and Loyalty to it.

In this early study of Voice behavior as a proxy of BOC, the argument has been supported **only** for negative behavioral commitment, namely, exit. This is not enough to confirm the core element of OC as unrewarded behavior. It supports employee behavior of event 1 (see Table 1), but not the expected behavior in event 3.

Chapter 9

Empirical Study II of BOC: EVLFN in Relation to Perceived Employment Alternatives and Perceived Organizational Power*

In this study, the relationships between the two new facets in the definition of organizational commitment (OC) is attempted by prediction of Facet F, behavioral organizational commitment (BOC), from Facet R (resources): perceived organizational power (POP) and perceived employment alternatives (PEA). While in the previous study, the measure BOC has been based on the original EVL model (1970), in this study, the measure uses the later elaborated model, which includes, in addition to Exit, Voice and Loyalty, the added categories of Neglect and Fence-sitting or Silence — EVLFN (see Chapter 2).

The effects of POP and PEA are tested on EVLFN as BOC. The commitment focus is the organization, as opposed to other foci, such as work groups or professions (Becker, 1992; Morrow, 1983). The organization is potentially a source of opportunities, gratification, threats and anxieties in

---

* Based on Bar-Haim (2007).

many ways, and the individual employee has two basic resources to secure his or her welfare: organizational power and employment alternatives. To some degree, these resources include all other securities and benefits.

People may perceive that they have high or low organizational power when they have a certain amount of formal power (authority) *and/or* a certain amount of informal power (influence). In addition, people may perceive their employment alternatives by reference to the worth of their personal human capital or occupational knowledge, skills and abilities (KSA) *and/or* to the opportunity structure in the labor market.

According to the old concepts of OC, in particular, the continuance or utilitarian base of commitment, the answer is clear: less organizational power and more alternatives should lead to lower OC because utilitarian value is built into the definition and measurement of OC. It is less obvious when OC is a behavior, not a set of interests, values, norms and sentiments.

Now recall the EVLFN categories:

1. Exit (active negative commitment)
2. Voice (active positive commitment)
3. Loyalty (passive positive commitment)
4. Fence-sitting or Silence (passive neutral commitment)
5. Neglect (passive negative commitment)

Two derived hypotheses are formulated about the relationships between BOC and POP and PEA as follows:

H1 (The conventional hypothesis): POP has a positive effect on BOC, whereas PEA has a negative effect. POP challenges employees and empowers, thus enhancing all types of positive or constructive commitment (Voice and Loyalty) and reducing all types of negative or destructive commitment (Exit, Neglect and Fence-sitting). On the other hand, PEA erodes OC through the propensity to avoid the cost of staying or of fighting for a change in a deteriorating organization.

H2 (A new hypothesis): Both POP and PEA are personal and non-organizational properties, which strengthen self-confidence and self-efficacy, enhance commitment and reduce escapism of all types, regardless of the exchange relationships between the organization and its employees. Therefore, there is no reason to assume that their effects will be different. The lack of any of them indicates weakness, and weak persons are less committed anyway.

The Study, Sample and Research Methods

The data for the study were drawn from the responses of 361 employees in Israel in four organized systems: a university, a medical center ($N = 46$), the Jewish Agency, a professional association and members of several dozen *Kibbutzim* (plural of *Kibbutz* — a communal village).

The dependent variable was measured by the following item: "Supposing that the department where you work gets into serious difficulties, due to any possible reason (academic problems, management failure, business problems, faulty human relations, etc.). What would be your reaction?":

1. Make any effort — above and beyond the call of my professional duty — to improve the situation (V).
2. Consider leaving this workplace (E).
3. Continue doing my work loyally and unquestioningly (L).
4. "Sit on the fence", weigh my options and continue performing loyally only the prescribed duties of my job (FS).
5. Perform the duties of my job, but in a less vigorous and conscientious manner than before (N).

The first factor, which accounts for most of the variance, is a bi-polar sequence, loaded high on constructive or positive commitment (Voice), and high (but with reverse signs) on negative or destructive commitment (Neglect and Fence-sitting). The other modes, Loyalty and Exit, are located between these poles, with Loyalty closer to Voice. Note that in this cognitive structure, Exit is not the most distant from Voice. This implies that employees, who are not actively committed to their workplace, may prefer to leave rather than stay to sit on the fence or even neglect their duties.

Table 1.   BOC Scale Based on EVLFN

Method 1: Factor analysis				Method 2: Guttman–Lingoes one-dimensional scaling[c]
Component	Eigenvalues[a]	% of Variance	Cumulative %	
1	1.808	36.161	36.161	
2	1.125	22.501	58.662	
Rotated component (factors)[b]				
Modes of BOC	1 — BOC scale		2 — Loyalty	
V — Voice	−0.798		−0.300	1.97 (1 — highest)
E — Exit	0.451		0.292	−0.51 (3)
L — Loyalty	−0.061		0.922	−0.16 (2)
N — Neglect	0.682		−0.275	−0.65 (4)
FS — Fence-sitting	0.707		−0.159	−0.65 (5 — lowest)

Notes: [a]Extraction method: Principal component.
[b]Rotation method: Varimax with Kaiser normalization.
[c]Goodness-of-fit (stress and alienation) = 0.

In a corroborative technique of smallest space analysis (Guttman–Lingoes multi-dimensional scaling), we see this elegant finding in the right column of Table 1. The one-dimensional order of the five modes of BOC is clear, as well as the relative distances separating them. Voice is farthest from all other rungs in the scale, and Exit again is not the worst mode of BOC. In fact, it comes after Loyalty and before Neglect.

In the second factor, we find Loyalty as the single significant loaded item. Since this factor is trivial (the original item can be used instead of the linear combination of all the items), it was ignored. However, note that this important item is not, of course, ignored or given up. It is given its due weight and included in the first factor.

Factor scores were calculated for the first factor that was labeled BOC scale, which serves as the dependent variable in this study.[1]

---

[1]Factor scores were multiplied by −1 to change the meaning of the values of this variable, namely, higher positive numbers express constructive or positive OC, and higher negative numbers express destructive or negative commitment.

The independent variables were POP and PEA. POP was measured by four items in a response to the following scenario: "Suppose that you wished to introduce changes into the department where you work, would you have sufficient resources of the following?":

1. Influence
2. Formal authority
3. Support of superiors
4. Support of peers

POP score was calculated as a count variable — POP is greater in as much as respondents indicate more items of organizational power. Thus, the range for POP is from 0 (NO to any of the four items — influence, authority, support of superiors and support of peers) up to 4 (YES to all items).

PEA was measured by three items in a response to the following scenario: "Suppose that you intended to leave your current job, would you have immediate other job opportunities?":

1. Yes, depending on my skills and abilities
2. Yes, depending on the current labor market conditions
3. Yes, depending on my skills and abilities, but not necessarily in the field of my experience

PEA is greater as respondents indicate more employment alternatives. The range for PEA is from 0 (NO to any of the three items — skills and abilities, labor market and skills and abilities, but not in the field of experience) up to 3 (YES to all items).

Plotting the BOC scale on POP and on PEA, and weighing these variables by length of service to control for its impact, we get two different patterns (see Figure 9.1): the BOC scale changes monotonically with POP and in a non-monotonic manner with PEA.[2] These patterns do not change

---

[2]Monotonic functions tend to move in only one direction as x increases. A monotonic increasing function always increases as x increases, $f(a) > f(b)$ for all $a > b$. A monotonic decreasing function always decreases as x increases, $f(a) < f(b)$ for all $a > b$.

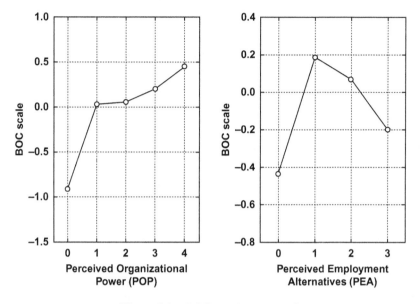

Figure 9.1.   BOC by POP and PEA[a]

Note: [a]Weighted by length of service.

even with no weighing by length of service. Therefore, the effect of length of service in this case is not significant.

For POP, the more the reports of influence, authority and support in the workplace, the more the reports of positive BOC in terms of Voice and Loyalty. For PEA, the picture is different: for zero PEA (14% of the sample), the BOC scale is low, actually a negative commitment. It soars to high positive commitment with one employment alternative, and then decreases, as more alternatives are perceived. It seems that people with no PEA do not have in mind any positive mode of OC. On the other hand, for those people who perceive some employment alternatives, OC is eroded steeply from positive BOC to negative BOC, perhaps in the direction of less active Voice and Loyalty and more Exit intentions (and to a smaller degree, also to Fence-sitting and Neglect).

Thus, the POP vector enhances positive BOC. However, the PEA vector moderates this force. We could make a reasonable guess that people with very high-perceived POP and PEA (0.6% of the sample — two employees) will express high positive BOC. On the other hand, it was also expected that people with very low-perceived POP and PEA (4.7% — 17 employees) will see themselves on the negative and perhaps destructive end of the BOC scale. However, what about the remaining majority located between these extremes of the commitment scale? By halving POP and PEA at their medians, and looking at the distributions of the five original items of commitment in each of the four cells of their cross-tabulation, we can see what happens to BOC under different conditions of POP and PEA (Table 2).

Employees with high POP and low PEA choose Voice and Loyalty by a significantly higher percentage, and Fence-sitting by a significantly lower percentage. On the other hand, people with high PEA and low POP choose Exit and Fence-sitting by a significantly higher percentage, and Voice by a significantly lower percentage. Cells 2 and 3 account for 118 cases and constitute a third of the sample.

What happens in other cells? In cell 4 (high POP and high PEA), which account for 58 cases, or 16% of the sample, Voice has been chosen by a significantly higher percentage in this cell, and all other modes of

Table 2. Distribution of BOC's items across POP and PEA[a]

Perceived employment alternatives (PEA)	Perceived organizational power (POP)		Total of BOC's items
	Low	High	
Low	**Cell 1**: ($N = 185$)	**Cell 2**: ($N = 73$)	($N = 361$)[b]
	$V = 63\%$	$V = 85\%$ (+)	$V = 70\%$
	$L = 38\%$	$L = 16\%$ (−)	$L = 32\%$
	$E = 14\%$	$E = 14\%$	$E = 18\%$
	$N = 10\%$	$N = 3\%$	$N = 7\%$
	FS $= 21\%$	FS $= 4\%$ (−)	FS $= 16\%$
High	**Cell 3**: ($N = 45$)	**Cell 4**: ($N = 58$)	
	$V = 56\%$ (−)	$V = 85\%$ (+)	
	$L = 40\%$	$L = 29\%$	
	$E = 44\%$ (+)	$E = 12\%$	
	$N = 2\%$	$N = 9\%$	
	FS $= 27\%$ (+)	FS $= 10\%$	

Notes: [a]Percentage significantly higher (+) or lower (−) than total according to χ^2 test.
[b]Percentages are for each item, not sum up to 100%.

commitment are similar to the raw total, with a slight tendency for a lower percentage of the negative modes of commitment. In cell 1 (low POP and low PEA), which comprises 185 persons, or 51% of the sample, no particular differences from the raw totals are discerned.

The arrangement of the commitment modes in four groups or "cells" reveals a complex picture. In fact, we find explanatory hints: some employees express behavioral constructive or destructive commitment tendencies, which are explained by exchange theories (cells 2 and 3); others show a commitment tendency with no apparent gains or interests (cell 1), or in spite of having organizational and employment alternatives (cell 4). This finding strengthens the guess that, in addition to the conventional wisdom of organizational and managerial thinking, BOC should be approached with more realistic and sophisticated understanding of the behavior of working people. Nevertheless, in this study, we were able to observe signs to event 3 in Table 1 of Chapter 8, namely, readiness of some employees to invest efforts to improve the system despite having occupational or income alternatives.

Chapter 10

Empirical Study III of BOC: Further Tests of the New Concept of Organizational Commitment

In this study, a twofold purpose is expected: (a) a more precise and direct measurement of behavioral organizational commitment (BOC) according to the mapping sentence, which includes an empirical mapping display of the entire space of the new definition of commitment, and (b) prediction of two forms of BOC by a larger set of predictors, including bases of OC (fact B).

The data is drawn from a survey among 316 respondents in five organizational settings[1]: tutors at the Open University of Israel, civil service employees in an HRM course, employees in a major NGO, employees in a mental health center and students in management studies in two colleges.

Part 1: Mapping the Relationships Among the Facets' Elements of the New Commitment Definition

Twelve items from a survey questionnaire were selected in line with the above mapping sentence and were analyzed according to principles of

---

[1] The same sample size as in study II is incidental.

55

facet analysis (Facet *C* has been omitted since the focus in this study is only on organizations, not individuals, groups or professions).[2]

Measurement

Forms of BOC constructed from two questions

A. Supposing that the organization for which you work gets into very serious difficulties, stops payment of wages and salaries on time, is on the brink of closing down, or is actually closed. What would be your reaction?

1. I would make every effort required under the circumstances, without immediate compensation and with no promise for compensation in the future, and willingly shoulder the burden of helping the organization to recover and return to normal activity.
2. I would make every effort required under the circumstances, without immediate compensation and with no promise of compensation in the future, and willingly shoulder the burden of helping the organization, at least for a while, though it is clear to me that it is doomed to ultimate failure.
3. I would stay in the organization as long as it stays operational and continue to loyally perform only the prescribed duties of my job.
4. I would leave the organization immediately, or at the first chance I get.
5. I would stay for a while in the organization, sit on the fence, weigh my options and continue performing only the minimum requirements.
6. I would stay in the organization because I have no choice, but evade my duties.

B. In the regular performance of your job, are you assigned difficult, unpleasant, stressful or boring tasks which are not specifically rewarded? How do you cope with these tasks?

1. No, I am not assigned unrewarded difficult, unpleasant, stressful or boring tasks.
2. Whenever I can, I attempt to evade difficult, unpleasant, stressful or boring tasks which are not specifically rewarded.

---

[2]Facet analysis is a wide field of research. A nice concise example is Guttman and Greenbaum (1998).

3. I perform them in a routine manner, as required by the formal job description, with no extra effort.
4. I make every effort to perform them to the best of my ability, and I find personal satisfaction in overcoming difficulties and frustrations at work.
5. I make every effort to perform them to the best of my ability, because they are part of my work duties, and duties must be performed.

Two variables of BOC were obtained as explained in the following.

Rewarded and Unrewarded BOC

1. No unrewarded commitment (categories 4– 6 in question A, or categories 1–3 in question B).
2. Performing unrewarded and unpleasant routine duties (category 3 in question A or 5 in question B).
3. Shouldering duties in troubled time to save the organization for no rewards (category 1 or 2 in question A).
4. Categories 2 + 3.

Unrewarded (Sisyphean) BOC

1. Non-Sisyphean OC (those who are not at level 2 in Rewarded and Unrewarded BOC).
2. Sisyphean BOC (levels 2–4 in item I, excluding all respondents with positive answers in bases of OC (see items 3.1, 3.2 and 3.3).
3. Bases of OC (Allen & Meyer's scales).
   3.1. Affective OC.
   3.2. Normative OC.
   3.3. Continuance OC.

Resources[3]

I. **Perceived employment alternatives (PEA)**: "In case you intend to leave your current job, will you have other immediate job opportunities?" 1 — Certainly No, 2 — No, 3 — I am not sure, 4 — Yes, 5 — Certainly Yes.

---

[3]Taken from study II with slightly wording modifications.

1. Depending on my skills and abilities.
2. Depending on the current labor market conditions.
3. Depending on my skills and abilities, but not necessarily in the field of my experience.

II. *Perceived organizational power (POP)*: "In case you wish to introduce changes into the department where you work, will you have sufficient of the following resources?" 1 — Certainly No, 2 — No, 3 — I am not sure, 4 — Yes, 5 — Certainly Yes.

1. Influence.
2. Formal power (authority).
3. Support of superiors.
4. Support of peers.

Statistical analysis

In Figure 10.1, the dispersion of the 12 items are presented graphically in a two-dimensional space, representing a matrix of non-parametric weak monotonicity correlations (MONCO) between the items, and a non-parametric mapping procedure of weighted smallest-space analysis (WSSA).[4]

Searching for a meaningful structure in this space diagram is done by a combination of heuristic considerations of the content of the items, and a mathematical search for the right regional location of the elements in the space diagram (see Figure 10.2). We obtain empirical dispersion of the commitment's items, which is arranged in a configuration called RADEX. This construct is, as we can see in Figure 10.2, a combination of two partitions of the space: an *axial* (or *angular*) partition with two regions and a *modular* (or *radial*) partition with two regions. Elements of a radial partition are ordered in concentric rings around an imagined origin, from the inner resources facet *R* to the outer forms of BOC facet *F*.

---

[4] Hebrew University Data Analysis Package (HUDAP), Release 8.0. In these techniques, the correlation matrix (in this case MONCO) is transformed into Euclidean distances, where the relative distances are smaller as far as the correlations are higher. Goodness-of-fit measure is 0.001.

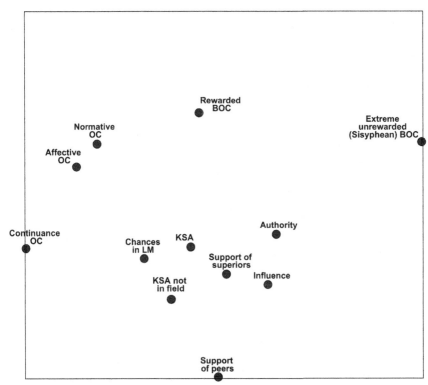

Figure 10.1. Mapping 12 Items of the Semantic Space of Organizational Commitment by WSSA

Note: LM = Labor Market; KSA = Knowledge, Skills and Abilities.

At the same time, elements of the axial partition are grouped in two parallel regions: personal versus organizational properties of the commitment phenomenon. Thus, in this WSSA solution, space is divided in four regions (see Figure 10.2): 1 — "Rewarded forms of OC", 2 — "Unrewarded forms of OC", 3 — "Personal resources" and 4 — "Organizational resources".

Figure 10.2 depicts the tentative conclusion about the relationships among the facets' elements of the new definition of organizational commitment.

This configuration implies that organizational commitment has at its core personal or organizational resources, which enable organizational commitment choices. These commitment choices, either personal

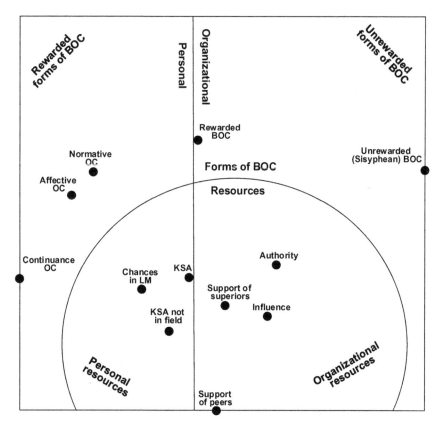

Figure 10.2. Facet Analysis of 12 Items of the Semantic Space of Organizational Commitment

or organizational, stem from or are dependent on this core. However, the extreme (Sisyphean) unrewarded OC is less related to any forms of BOC or resources. Perhaps with more research, we may be able to understand the rarely researched organizational commitment, as a behavior of "stay or leave". We may discover complex reasons for it, but what we have already seen in this small study are signs that this behavior is more than exchange relationships between employees and their employing organizations. For some working people, organizational commitment is a *raison d'être* no less powerful than a contractual relationship.

Part 2: Predicting Organizational Commitment as Unrewarded Behavior

In this part, I intend to refine and elaborate the new measure of BOC and show its strength and weakness *vis-à-vis* older OC measures that are based on attitudes and motives of organizational commitment but not behaviors.

Method

I use categorical regression (CATREG) to predict BOC by a set of variables from the new mapping sentence of organizational commitment and its close domains.[5]

Dependent variables

Rewarded and Unrewarded BOC and unrewarded (Sisyphean) BOC as defined above in part 1.

Independent variables

Six groups of independent variables (comprise 19 variables) were measured, as follows:

I. *Bases of OC (according to Allen & Meyer's scales)*:

1. Affective OC — **Mean: 5.02, SD: 1.02** (range: 1–7).
2. Normative OC — **Mean: 4.71, SD: 0.94** (range: 1–7).
3. Continuance OC — **Mean: 4.18, SD: 1.06** (range: 1–7).

II. *General attitudes*:

1. Values scale (based on the typology of McDonald and Gandz (1991) and the questionnaire that Finegan (2000) developed. It indicates the

---

[5]The use of CATREG, developed by Data Theory Scaling System Group (DTSS), Faculty of Social and Behavioral Sciences Leiden University, the Netherlands, and SPSS, is because it can handle nominal, ordinal or numerical variables in the same regression through optimal scaling techniques.

degree of importance of values in the respondent's life)[6] — **Mean: 4.15, SD: 0.34** (range: 1–5).

2. Fair rewards ("Do you receive fair wages and satisfactory rewards for your efforts on behalf of the organization for which you work?") — **Mean: 2.84, SD: 0.94** (range: 1–5).

III. Perceived employment alternatives:

1. As much as it depends on my skills and abilities — **Mean: 3.57, SD: 0.93**.
2. As much as it depends on the current labor market conditions — **Mean: 3.29, SD: 0.92**.
3. As much as it depends on my skills and abilities, but not necessarily in the field of my experience — **Mean: 3.66, SD: 0.88**.

IV. *Perceived organizational power*:

1. Influence — **Mean: 3.28, SD: 1.17**.
2. Formal power (authority) — **Mean: 3.48, SD: 1.14**.
3. Support of superiors — **Mean: 4.0, SD: 0.92**.
4. Support of peers — **Mean: 2.61, SD: 1.31**.

V. *Organizational size*: (Workforce size: 1–299 (**69%**); 300–999 (**19%**); 1000+ (**12%**).

VI. *Personal characteristics*:

1. Length of service (in years) — **Mean: 7.74, SD: 5.27**.
2. Age — **Mean: 39.55, SD: 9.82**.
3. Non-tenure job — 1 — in a full-time tenured job (**51%**), 2 — in part-time tenured job (**18%**), 3 — in full-time personal contract — no tenure (**16%**), 4 — in part-time personal contract — no tenure (**15%**).
4. Gender — 1 — man (**24%**), 2 — woman (**76%**).
5. Schooling (in years of learning) — **Mean: 14.91, SD: 2.82**.
6. Education — 1 — high school or less (**15%**), 2 — tertiary education (**21%**), 3 — academic (**64%**).

---

[6] I use a single measure of Values scale (average score on 24 items of Finegan's questionnaire, on a range of "1 Very Unimportant" to "5 Very Important"). I failed to reproduce the factor structure of Finegan in my data. However, even her data yield poor reliability scores (*ibid*, p. 157), and according to the theory of OC that I attempt to develop, what matters is not the different types and dimensions of personal values, but the propensity to appreciate values in life.

Findings

Table 1 shows the results of predicting rewarded and unrewarded BOC. The overall model is significant and has considerable prediction power. The significant effects (betas) are marked and inform: (a) positive impact of affective OC, perceived power of influence and support of peers (as far as respondents have affective base of OC and perceived influence and support of peers, they are more inclined to rewarded and unrewarded BOC);

Table 1. CATREG-dependent: Rewarded and Unrewarded BOC (Mean: 2.32; SD: 0.99)

Multiple R	R square	Adjusted R square	Regression mean square	F	Sig.
0.563	0.318	0.125	1.453	1.650	0.027

	Standardized coefficients				
Independent variables	Beta	Std. error	df	F	Sig.
Affective OC	0.265	0.104	1	6.537	0.012
Normative OC	−0.051	0.091	1	0.312	0.578
Continuance OC	0.118	0.101	1	1.369	0.244
Values	−0.062	0.091	1	0.461	0.499
Fair rewards	0.129	0.081	3	2.541	0.060
Skills and abilities	0.123	0.088	2	1.939	0.148
Current labor market	0.151	0.081	1	3.488	0.064
Skills and abilities not in field	−0.262	0.094	3	7.698	0.000
Influence	0.230	0.108	3	4.536	0.005
Authority	−0.109	0.112	3	0.947	0.421
Support of superiors	0.190	0.089	1	4.577	0.034
Support of peers	0.024	0.106	1	0.049	0.825
Workforce size	−0.106	0.113	1	0.891	0.347
Length of service	−0.134	0.092	1	2.101	0.150
Age	0.161	0.082	1	3.827	0.053
Non-tenure job	0.074	0.093	1	0.644	0.424
Gender	0.058	0.088	1	0.436	0.511
Schooling	−0.169	0.104	5	2.652	0.026
Education	0.116	0.106	2	1.201	0.305

(b) negative impact of perceived alternatives in finding a new job not in the field of experience (as far as respondents assess their ability to find such a job, they are less inclined to rewarded and unrewarded BOC); (c) age increases the tendency to rewarded and unrewarded BOC, and number of years of schooling decreases it.

Table 2 shows the results of predicting extreme (Sisyphean) unrewarded BOC. The overall model is significant and has even stronger

Table 2.   CATREG-dependent: Unrewarded (Sisyphean) BOC (Mean: 0.07; SD: 0.26)

Multiple R	R square	Adjusted R square	Regression mean square	F	Sig.
0.692	0.478	0.331	2.188	3.249	0.000

	Standardized coefficients				
Independent variables	Beta	Std. error	df	F	Sig.
Affective OC	−0.168	0.092	1	3.364	0.069
Normative OC	−0.372	0.085	1	19.277	0.000
Continuance OC	−0.342	.088	1	15.175	0.000
Values	0.032	0.079	1	0.168	0.682
Fair rewards	−0.242	0.069	3	12.315	0.000
Skills and abilities	0.168	0.084	3	4.028	0.009
Current labor market	−0.147	0.072	2	4.194	0.017
Skills and abilities not in field	−0.147	0.079	1	3.477	0.065
Influence	0.100	0.083	3	1.458	0.230
Authority	0.124	0.101	3	1.525	0.212
Support of superiors	−0.050	0.085	2	0.344	0.709
Support of peers	−0.065	0.089	1	0.545	0.462
Workforce size	−0.053	0.095	1	0.311	0.578
Length of service	0.098	0.079	1	1.559	0.214
Age	0.074	0.078	1	0.903	0.344
Non-tenure job	0.136	0.081	1	2.787	0.098
Gender	0.055	0.076	1	0.516	0.474
Schooling	−0.228	0.077	5	8.724	0.000
Education	−0.097	0.082	1	1.413	0.237

prediction power than that for rewarded and unrewarded BOC. However, the pattern of significant betas is different, as follows: (a) negative impact of normative and continuance OC (as far as respondents have normative and continuance bases of OC, they are less inclined to Sisyphean unrewarded BOC)[7]; (b) negative impact of fair rewards (as respondents assess that their rewards are fair, they are less inclined to Sisyphean unrewarded BOC); (c) PEA of skills and abilities in finding a new job has a positive impact on Sisyphean unrewarded BOC, while favorability of current labor market has a negative one; (d) as in the analysis of rewarded and unrewarded BOC, there is a negative impact of schooling on Sisyphean unrewarded BOC.

Among the personal characteristics, only schooling has any (negative) effect on behavior of unrewarded commitment. Also, the PEA and perceived organizational power do not reveal a consistent pattern of explanation for the moderate rewarded and unrewarded BOC and even less for the extreme unrewarded BOC. On the other hand, the affective and normative bases of commitment and fair rewards, with their negative effects on unrewarded BOC and their considerable portion of the explained variance (not displayed), strengthen the assertion about the uniqueness of unrewarded BOC.

The results of the presented small studies here are mixed in regard to the importance of the new facet of resources in the redefinition of the concept of organizational commitment. We need many more studies to evaluate this facet, and of course to update and refine the new mapping sentence. However, the heart of the changed concept, namely, the behavioral forms of organizational commitment, receives consistent support, both qualitatively, as in the facet analysis above, and, quantitatively, as in the regression analyses.

---

[7] These inverse relationships are partly due to the definition and measurement of extreme (Sisyphean) BOC, namely, the exclusion of positive answers on Allen & Meyer's scales.

Chapter 11

Epistemological View of Organizational Commitment

Everyone has multiple commitments. Of these, some commitments are routine with well-defined terms and well-protected measures against infringement, such as bank loans. For this type of commitment, I have no specific theory of behavior and it is well explained and theorized in other disciplines, such as economics, sociology and psychology.

However, I try to explain the less-defined, non-routine commitment. Some of these commitments are tolerable and some are unpleasant. This book is mainly about difficult, unpleasant, sometimes intolerable and agonizing commitments. Everyone would prefer to get rid of such commitments, and occasionally, it is possible. You might overlook an obligation, ignore it, escape it and you may not be punished, or pay less than it takes to infringe it. This is true especially for unspecified, non-routine commitments, such as in personal relationships, social associations, political parties and religious communities. In these cases, loyalty and commitment to act on behalf of the social unit often lack formal obligations, specified timetables and particular sanctions to show performance. These features epitomize commitments to family, congregational communities, political parties and many other voluntarist associations.

Non-routine commitments are characterized by long-range timetable and low probability of the requirement to fulfil them. The most conspicuous example is the commitment to stay married for life. But life commitment in other social frameworks such as workplace, religious community or political party have also been widely observed. In personal, group, social, political, religious and national systems of relationships, unrestricted commitment in time is often demanded, with strong emphasis on loyalty, help in troubled times and situations, and staying, not deserting. This demand is not anchored only in the emotional basis of identification, agreement and love, which are essential but not sufficient.

Great amount of efforts and resources are invested in internalization, education and enforcement of the norm of staying and not leaving in times of difficulties and troubles. Sometimes, securing commitment is done by creating risks of loss of accumulated assets and benefits and by formal contracts to deter escape from commitment.

However, the non-routine, long-term commitments are different from simple well-defined commitment to pay back a loan. The sanction in the latter case is clear and the financial behavior is quite predictable. On the other hand, the commitment to give up life in defending the country is less defined and less predictable. For example, escape from the battle field because of fear is not always an act of high treason. Relative to numerous such escapes, only few soldiers were executed for treachery.

Even a wife's leaving a husband with Alzheimer's disease in a decent shelter, after many years of togetherness, is not necessarily a breach of her vows as a young woman to stay with him in health and sickness. Thus, how can we know with a reasonable confidence, who will remain loyal to his undetermined long-term commitments, when we cannot specify the conditions of the critical event of the requested commitment?

Another type of unspecified commitment is often a declaration of intended commitment to some goals or values by managers and leaders of organizations and institutions. Actually, it is not a commitment at all, but an intention, which lacks specific conditions of realization.

So far, three types of commitment have been identified: (a) routine, based on economic, social and psychological reasons, and with specific characteristics of time range, costs and sanctions for failure to comply; (b) non-routine, with no specific time range and concrete required actions, and no formal sanctions in failure to comply; (c) a commitment declaration, which is not a real commitment.

And what type is the organizational commitment (OC) that has been explored and practiced for more than 50 years? It is none of the above three. It deals with emotional, normative and utilitarian bases or anchors of commitment to organizations, not the commitment itself, which remains enigmatic to a large degree. Especially, in its extreme form of unrewarded behavior, namely, with no connection to any of the OC bases and resources.

This Sisyphean unrewarded behavior is unusual in any system, which is based on mutuality or exchange. It is not a metabolic system, and it is certainly not an altruistic behavior, which is always rewarded in some respect.[1] So, let us go back to the term "Sisyphean". It is used to denote an extreme case where employees work hard for no reward whatsoever, even not for the gratification of working for a workplace that you love or with whose goals and missions you identify, or the satisfaction that stems from the recognition that you are acting according to your social values and beliefs. I was influenced by and also borrowed from the great French author and philosopher Albert Camus this notion of extreme commitment in his essay, *The Myth of Sisyphus*. In this composition, he re-examines Sisyphus's apparently unrewarded, hard and useless task of pushing a rock uphill, only to have it roll down again, as rewarding and meaningful work for him, because only he is the autonomous and sovereign authority to decide what is meaningful and rewarding in his life.[2] *The Myth of Sisyphus* by Albert Camus inspired my thesis on OC as unrewarded behavior.

Camus opens his essay by claiming that "[t]here is but one truly serious philosophical problem and that is suicide. Judging whether life is or

---

[1] I have attempted to explain this unrewarded behavior by the well-known biological mechanism of handicap principle among certain species of birds, but my expert colleague rejected this brave trial. She even rejected the birds' behavior as a manifestation of altruism. On the contrary, she patiently explained: their *behavior* is an exhibition of selfish machoism.

[2] Albert Camus was born in Mondovi, Algeria on 1913. He published his first, and most famous, novel *The Outsider* in 1942. *The Myth of Sisyphus*, a philosophical essay, was published a year later, and was followed by novels like *The Fall* and *The Rebel*. In 1957, Camus was awarded the Nobel Prize for Literature. He died on January 4, 1960, in an automobile accident.

is not worth living amounts to answering the fundamental question of philosophy. All the rest ... comes afterward."

He reinterprets the Greek myth on Sisyphus, who is condemned by the gods to an endless futile task of ceaselessly rolling a rock to the top of a mountain, from where the stone would fall back. For Camus, current standards that gave meaning to the world and to the human life are not available to the "clear-thinking modern man". When one confronts the world intelligibly, he can find no meaning; the universe is silent to his desire for meaning. The lack of such an ultimate unifying principle or entity forces us to accept that all is absurd.

The absurdity of life must lead to answer negatively the question "Is life worth living?", and suicide thus becomes a logical alternative. The alternative of hope is also rejected by Camus because it is an unproven solution. However, Camus rejects the option of suicide because it is an escape from, rather than a solution to, the problem. The absurd is the only truth, the essence of human condition. Therefore, the proper alternative is to live with it. The value of life is its preservation in order to maintain the absurd polarity between humans and the world. This value is created by humans, and enhances humans' place in the universe as creators of values. In this way, Camus constructs an ethics and repudiates nihilism.

Thus, we can see why Camus thinks of Sisyphus as the ideal example of the absurd man. "His scorn of the gods, his hatred of death, and his passion for life won him the unspeakable penalty in which the whole being is exerted towards accomplishing nothing. That is the price that must be paid for the passions of this earth." But Camus assures us that Sisyphus is happy: "All Sisyphus' silent joy is contained therein. His fate belongs to him ... If there is a personal fate, there is no higher destiny, or at least there is, but one which he concludes is inevitable and despicable. For the rest, he knows himself to be the master of his days. At that subtle moment when man glances backward over his life, Sisyphus returning toward his rock, in that slight pivoting he contemplates that series of unrelated actions which become his fate, created by him, combined under his memory's eye and soon sealed by his death. Thus, convinced of the wholly human origin of all that is human, a blind man eager to see who knows that the night has no end, he is still on the go. The rock is still rolling ... I leave Sisyphus at the foot of the mountain! One always finds one's burden again. But Sisyphus teaches the higher fidelity that negates the gods and raises rocks. He too concludes that all is well. This universe henceforth without a master seems to him neither sterile nor futile. Each atom of that stone, each mineral flake of that night filled mountain, in itself forms a world. The struggle itself toward the heights is enough to fill a man's heart. One must imagine Sisyphus happy."

Camus' Sisyphus is perhaps the ideal type of a committed employee if she/he is making unrewarded extra efforts on behalf of the employing organization, or performing unrewarded unpleasant routine duties or unrewarded shouldering of duties in troubled time to save the employing organization. From an external point of view, it is absurd, but from the committed person's point of view, it is the utmost autonomy to give consciously or unconsciously meaning to her/his working life. All other forms of relationships and exchange between employees and their work organizations are governed by other well-explained economic, sociological and psychological mechanisms and dynamics.

But let us take the Devil's advocate's stance against the thesis here. He may argue the following view: If I understand your challenge on the current concept of OC, we are dealing with a person in her or his workplace as a well-defined entity, and this person has emotional, cognitive and behavioral attitudes towards this entity. These attitudes may result in OC that can be observed or be examined only in certain situations (serious personal or organizational disasters). In these situations, the employed person will persevere in his work and will invest a lot of unrewarded efforts even if she/he have alternative better occupational options elsewhere. You claim that this behavioral manifestation of OC is dichotomous: staying in the working organization, which is in troubles, or leaving it to a better workplace to secure his or her livelihood. Therefore, OC is a synonym word for loyalty to the employing organization, and its test is in troubled times. A similar description of OC that comes to my mind is that of football club's ultras, who do not abandon their club, despite a long series of losing games, sometimes through many years, because they are attached their club. For them and for many honest and conscientious owners, managers and workers with good will and good intentions, you bring sad tidings.

I wonder (the Devil's advocate) why you insist on the dichotomy of this commitment behavior, namely, staying or leaving? Perhaps, there are more intermediate behavioral modes of commitment between staying and leaving. In fact, you suggest additional forms of behavioral organizational commitment (BOC) in your above studies, either in the EVLFN scale in study II, or in the BOC scale in study III.

Finally, even if I take your argument that BOC is out of managers' control, they cannot train for it or encourage it because it is a unique inner quality of the few of their workforce. Perhaps, these few employees themselves are not aware of this quality in normal times in their working life. Nevertheless, is it possible to identify and preselect such employees by human resource management (HRM) selection tests?

What Shall I Answer to the Devil's Advocate?

The need to reformulate the concept of OC, I hope, has been evident both epistemologically and empirically. However, I have no intention to throw out the baby with the bathwater. The psychological, sociological and economic bases of OC, and the foci of OC are valid and make sense in many scenes of OC. Let us go back to the relationships between love and commitment: you can love your spouse for a million of reasons, and yet show behaviors of commitment by applying acts of responsibility and paying off obligations for her/him. This is an example of affection-based commitment. However, this or other bases of committed behaviors are not part of the commitment behavior itself. Thus, the new definition of OC includes both the rewarded and unrewarded behaviors of OC.

But the most difficult matter to explain in my theory about OC and yet the most enigmatic one is its unrewarded dimension. I already have noted above that I could not find an example of voluntary human or non-human unrewarded behavior. The handicap principle among certain birds as an altruistic behavior that I tried to use was rejected in favor of its opposite, a machoism behavior of the male birds and other living species. We also know that altruism in the social sciences, in general, and in organizational behavior, in particular, is a well-rewarded behavior in many ways. So, OC cannot be equated neither with the handicap principle nor with altruism.

The problem of the concept of unrewarded behavior is not confined to altruism. It is much wider because it infringes on a basic principle of exchange relationships in systems theory in general and open systems theory in particular. As it is well known, any system — biological, physical, social, economic, cultural and political — is located in certain environments and is dependent for its survival on resources from these environments. Though, according to Piaget (1970, p. 5), a system is a self-regulated structure of mutual interactions or transformations among its elements, any living system is not absolute self-regulatory or autonomous. It needs to maintain exchange relationships with its environment to get required resources and to contribute back valuable outputs to the environment. Katz and Kahn (1978) already defined the properties of such open living systems in the social sciences, including organizational systems. Among these properties, we find clear boundaries, hierarchy, negative entropy (that indicates positive balance of exchange with the environment), feedback mechanisms, growth by elaboration and differentiation and equifinality (the principle that the living system's goals can be reached by many ways).

When we go back to the state of working organizations that are in trouble, we may find that some or most critical features of their system are disrupted or even paralyzed and, therefore, they are unable to contribute value to their critical environments, such as suppliers, clients, creditors, regulators, or employees. So, what is interrupted in these situations is the exchange mechanism, and I allegedly suggest in my thesis on OC a bypass or contradicting phenomenon to mutuality and exchange in living systems, which seems to be a law of Nature.

Let us take one feature of living systems: negative entropy. In Nature, entropy is a thermodynamic feature representing the lack of a system's energy for conversion into mechanical work and often is interpreted as the degree of disorder or gradual decline into disorder in the system. We may interpret any living system as a struggle against entropic forces, which sooner or later is doomed to fail.

Thus, I do not claim that there is a way to avoid organizational severe crises by the commitment of few unrewarded employees. What is unique about the features of BOC is that in the general chaos of the disrupted exchange processes in the organization in crisis and in the relationships with its environments or stakeholders, those with extreme Sisyphean behavioral commitment are less affected because they are more autonomous than other sectors of the employing organization (managers and other workers). Apparently, they have in mind different living priorities that have been dormant until they have to face the difficulties of their workplace. Besides, they have had this unique autonomy in normal times of the employing organization, when they were performing unrewarded difficult, unpleasant, stressful or boring duties, which are not part of their employment contract.

Therefore, at the level of the individual worker, unrewarded OC is reserved for those employees who will give their efforts, skills and abilities in lasting rough situations without taking anything back. This is possible not forever, but for long time enough to notice that this phenomenon, which is the legacy of *The Few*, does not infringe on the exchange principle of systems. On the contrary, in infrequent times, exchange imperatives do not help systems to survive because chaotic forces disrupt the normal sense-making of the system's behavior. In chaotic states, such as severe fires, battlefields or a major medical surgery that has been become complicated, rare persons take risks to overcome the crisis that are against their own safety, often against the rules of the system, which are aimed to minimize additional damage and loss of life.

As for the tidings, it is sad for employing organizations and for their leaders in particular (owners and managers). However, I hope that I have conveyed convincingly their stance in the real world of work today. Most of them do not care about their workforce. They escape from social responsibility, and they do not believe any more in the connection between OC and organizational and business performance.

You may wonder if there are selection methods of human resource management (HRM) to discover and select the behaviorally committed employees in general and the unrewarded ones in particular. It is still an open question. Currently, I do not know about any selection system that can identify "behaviorally committed employees". However, there is no reason to assume that it is not possible. Now, we can explain, "predict" to a certain degree, behavioral organizational commitment (BOC). Still, this behavior is enigmatic.

Concluding Remark

Behavioral organizational commitment (BOC) is substantially a superior concept to organizational commitment (OC). It better explains the unique meaning of commitment in the real world of work, which nowadays is escaping from any OC toward employees, in particular, and any responsibility toward other stakeholders, in general.

Symbolically, the few workers in the extreme category of unrewarded BOC, according to my studies so far, are the "Lamed Vav Tzadikim"[1] of the employing organization. They are prepared to stay and help their workplace for no rewards, and they cannot tell why.

---

[1] Refers to the 36 righteous people who save the world, according to the tradition of Judaism.

References

Akdogan, A. and Cingoz, A. (2009). The effects of organizational downsizing and layoffs on organizational commitment: A field research. *Journal of American Academy of Business*. 14(2), 337–343.

Allen, N. J. and Meyer, J. P. (1990). The measurement and antecedents of affective, continuance and normative commitment to the organization. *Journal of Occupational Psychology*. 63, 1–18.

Anderson, E. (1988). Transaction costs as determinants of opportunism in integrated and independent sales forces. *Journal of Economic Behavior and Organization*. 9, 247–264.

Anderson, E. and Weitz, B. (1992). The use of pledges to build and sustain commitment in distribution channels. *Journal of Marketing Research*. 25, 18–34.

Axelrod, R. (1984). *The Evolution of Cooperation*. New York: Basic Books.

Bar-Haim, A. (2007). Rethinking organizational commitment in relation to perceived organizational power and perceived employment alternatives. *International Journal of Cross Cultural Management*. 7(2), 203–217.

Bar-Hayim, A. and Berman, G. S. (1992). The dimensions of organizational commitment. *Journal of Organizational Behavior*. 13, 379–387.

Bar-Haim, A. and Harnoy, H. (2009). Essence and techniques in redefinition of the concept of organizational commitment (OC). *Effective Executive*. 12(11), 52–57.

Baruch, Y. (1998). The rise and fall of organizational commitment. *Human Systems Management*. 17(2), 135–143.

Becker, H. S. (1960). Notes on the concept of commitment. *American Journal of Sociology.* 66, 32–42.

Blau, G. J. and Boal, K. B. (1987). Conceptualizing how job involvement and organizational commitment affect turnover and absenteeism. *Academy of Management Review.* 12, 288–300.

Borg, I. (1990). Multiple facetisations of work values. *Applied Psychology: An International Review.* 39, 401–412.

Boroff, K. E. and Lewin, D. (1997). Loyalty, voice, and intent to exit a union firm: A conceptual and empirical analysis. *Industrial & Labor Relations Review.* 51(1), 50–63.

Burton, J. P., Lee, T. W. and Holtom, B. C. (2002). The influence of motivation to attend, ability to attend, and organizational commitment on different types of absence behaviors. *Journal of Managerial Issues.* 14(2), 181–197.

Caldwell, D. F. and O'Reilly, C. A. (1990). Measuring person-job fit with a profile comparison process. *Journal of Applied Psychology.* 75, 648–657.

Cohen, A. (1993). Organizational commitment and turnover: A meta-analysis. *Academy of Management Journal.* 36, 1140–1157.

Cohen, E. H. (2000). A facet theory approach to examining overall life satisfaction relationships. *Social Indicators Research.* 51(2), 223–234.

Cohen, A. and Lowenberg, G. (1990). Reexamination of the side-bet theory as applied to organizational commitment: A meta-analysis. *Human Relations.* 43(10), 1015–1050.

Cook, J. D. and Wall, T. D. (1980). New work attitude measures of trust, organizational commitment, and personal need non fulfillment. *Journal of Occupational Psychology.* 53, 39–52.

Dose, J. J. (1997). Work values: An integrative framework and illustrative application to organizational socialization. *Journal of Occupational and Organizational Psychology.* 70, 219–240.

Dwyer, F. R., Schurr, P. and Oh, S. (1987). Developing buyer/seller relationships. *Journal of Marketing.* 51, 11–27.

Edwards, J. R. (1994). The study of congruence in organizational behaviour research: Critique and a proposed alternative. *Organizational Behaviour and Human Decision Processes.* 58, 51–100.

Elizur, D. (1984). Facets of work values: A structural analysis of work outcomes. *Journal of Applied Psychology.* 69, 379–389.

England, G. (1975). *The Manager and his Values: An International Perspective.* Cambridge, MA: Ballinger.

England, G. and Lee, R. (1974). The relationship between managerial values and managerial success in the United States, Japan, India and Australia. *Journal of Applied Psychology.* 59, 411–419.

Farrell, D. (1983). Exit, voice, loyalty and neglect as responses to job dissatisfaction: A multidimensional scaling study. *Academy of Management Journal.* 26(3), 596–606.

Farzaneh, J., Dehghanpour, F. A. and Kazemi, M. (2014). The impact of person-job fit and person-organization fit on OCB. *Personnel Review.* 43(5), 672–691.

Finegan, J. E. (2000). The impact of person and organizational values on organizational commitment. *Journal of Occupational and Organizational Psychology.* 73(2), 149–169.

Fishbein, M. and Ajzen, I. (1975). *Beliefs, Attitudes, Intention, and Behavior.* MA: Addison-Wesley.

Frazier, G. L. and Rody, R. C. (1991). The use of influence strategies in inter firm relationships in industrial product channels. *Journal of Marketing.* 55(1), 52–69.

Gouldner, A. W. (1960). The norm of reciprocity: A preliminary statement. *American Sociological Review.* 25, 161–179.

Guttman, R. and Greenbaum, C. W. (1998). Facet theory: Its development and current status. *European Psychologist.* 3(1), 13–36.

Heide, J. B. and John, G. (1992). Do norms matter in marketing relationships? *Journal of Marketing.* 56, 32–44.

Hirschman, A. O. (1970). *Exit, Voice, and Loyalty.* Cambridge, MA: Harvard University Press.

Ho, W.-H., Chang, C. S., Shih, Y.-L. and Liang, R.-D. (2009). Effects of job rotation and role stress among nurses on job satisfaction and organizational commitment. *BMC Health Services Research.* 9,8, doi:10.1186/1472-6963-9-8.

Jackson, B. B. (1985). *Winning and Keeping Industrial Customers.* Lexington, MA: Lexington Books.

John, G. and Weitz, B. (1989). Salesforce compensation: An empirical investigation of factors related to use of salary versus incentive compensation. *Journal of Marketing Research.* 26, 1–14.

Joshi, A. W. and Stump, R. L. (1999). Determinants of commitment and opportunism: Integrating and extending insights from transaction cost analysis and relational exchange theory. *Revue Canadienne des Sciences de l'Administration*. 4, 334–352.

Kanter, R. M. (1972). *Commitment and Community: Communes and Utopias in Sociological Perspective*. Cambridge, MA: Harvard University Press.

Katz, D. and Kahn, R. L. (1978). *The Social Psychology of Organizations*, 2nd edn. Wiley.

Keisuke, K. (2018). Education, organizational commitment, and rewards within Japanese manufacturing companies in China. *Employee Relations*. 40(3), 458–485.

Kelman, H. C. (1958). Compliance, identification, and internalization: Three processes of attitude change. *Journal of Conflict Resolution*. 2(1), 51–60.

Kim, K. Y., Eisenberger, R. and Baik, K. (2016). Perceived organizational support and affective organizational commitment: Moderating influence of perceived organizational competence. *Journal of Organizational Behavior*. 37(4), 558–583.

Kristof, A. L. (1996). Person-organization fit: An integrative review of its conceptualizations, measurement, and implications. *Personnel Psychology*. 49, 1–49.

Lachman, R. and Noy, S. (1996). Reactions of salaried physicians to hospital decline. *Health Services Research*. 31(2), 171–190.

Luthans, F., McCaul, H. S. and Dodd, N. G. (1985). Organizational commitment: A comparison of American, Japanese, and Korean employees. *Academy of Management Journal*. 28(1), 213–219.

Macneil, I. R. (1980). *The New Social Contract: An Inquiry into Modern Contractual Relations*. New Haven, CT: Yale University Press.

Mathiew, J. E. and Zajac, D. M. (1990). A review and meta-analysis of the antecedents, correlations and consequences of organizational commitment. *Psychological Bulletin*. 108(2), 171–194.

McDonald, P. (1993). Individual-organizational value congruence: Operationalization and consequents. Unpublished Doctoral Dissertation. London, ON, Canada: University of Western Ontario.

McDonald, P. and Gandz, J. (1991). Identification of values relevant to business research. *Human Resource Management*. 30, 217–236.

McDonald, P. and Gandz, J. (1992). Getting value from shared values. *Organisational Dynamics.* 20, 64–77.

Meyer, J. P. and Allen, N. J. (1997). *Commitment in the Workplace: Theory, Research and Application.* Thousand Oaks, CA: Sage.

Meyer, J., Becker, T. and Vandenberghe, C. (2004). Employee commitment and motivation: A conceptual analysis and integrative model. *Journal of Applied Psychology.* 89, 991–1007.

Mowday, R., Steers, R. and Porter, L. (1979). The measurement of organizational commitment. *Journal of Vocational Behavior.* 14, 224–227.

Near, J. P. (1989). Organizational commitment among Japanese and U.S. workers. *Organization Studies.* 10(3), 281–300.

O'Reilly, C. A., III and Chatman, J. (1986). Organizational commitment and psychological attachment: The effects of compliance, identification, and internalization on pro-social behavior. *Journal of Applied Psychology.* 71, 492–499.

O'Reilly, C. A., Chatman, J. and Caldwell, D. F. (1991). People and organizational culture: A profile comparison approach to assessing person-organization fit. *Academy of Management Journal.* 34, 487–516.

Penley, L. E. and Gould, S. (1988). Etzioni's model of organizational involvement: A perspective for understanding commitment to organizations. *Journal of Organizational Behavior.* 9, 43–59.

Piaget, J. (1970). *Structuralism.* New York: Basic Books.

Posner, B. Z. (1992). Person-organization value congruence: No support for individual differences as a moderating influence. *Human Relations.* 45, 351–361.

Powell, W. W. (1990). Neither market nor hierarchy: Network forms of organization. In Staw, B. M. and Cummings, L. L. (Eds.), *Research in Organizational Behavior,* Vol. 12. Greenwich, CT: JAI Press, pp. 295–336.

Randall, D. M., Fedor, D. B. and Longenecker, C. O. (1990). The behavioral expression of organizational commitment. *Journal of Vocational Behavior.* 36, 210–224.

Rokeach, M. (1973). *The Nature of Human Values.* New York: Free Press.

Rusbult, C. E. and Fan-ell, D. (1983). A longitudinal test of the investment model: The impact on job satisfaction, job commitment, and turnover of variations in rewards, costs, alternatives, and investments. *Journal of Applied Psychology.* 68, 429–438.

Rusbult, C. E., Farrell, D., Rogers, G. and Mainous, A. G., III (1988). Impact of exchange variables on exit, voice, loyalty, and neglect: An integrative model of responses to declining job satisfaction. *Academy of Management Journal.* 1(3), 599–627.

Rusbult, C. E., Johnson, D. J. and Morrow, G. D. (1986). Determinants and consequences of exit, voice, loyalty, and neglect: Responses to dissatisfaction in adult romantic involvements. *Human Relations.* 39(1), 45–63.

Salancik, G. R. (1977). Commitment and the control of organizational behavior and belief. In: Staw, B. M. and Salancik, G. R. (Eds.). *New Directions in Organizational Behavior.* Chicago: St. Clair Press.

Schappe, S. P. (1998). The influence of job satisfaction, organizational commitment, and fairness perceptions on organizational citizenship behavior. *The Journal of Psychology.* 132(3), 277–290.

Schrader, B. (2010). Industrial/organizational psychology 2010: A research odyssey. In Halonen, J. S. and Davis, S. F. (Eds.). *The Many Faces of Psychological Research in the 21st Century.* Retrieved from the Society for the Teaching of Psychology, http://teachpsych.org/ebooks/faces/index_faces.php.

Schwartz, S. H. and Bilsky, W. (1987). Toward a universal psychological structure of human values. *Journal of Personality and Social Psychology.* 53, 550–562.

Seligman, C. and Katz, A. N. (1996). Dynamics of value systems. In Seligman, C., Olson, J. M. and Zanna, M. P. (Eds.), *Psychology of Values: The Ontario Symposium*, Vol. 8. Hillsdale, NJ: Erlbaum, pp. 1–24.

Tan, D. S. K. and Akhtar, S. (1998). Organizational commitment and experienced burnout: An exploratory study from a Chinese cultural perspective. *International Journal of Organizational Analysis.* 6(4), 310–333.

Turnley, W. H. and Feldman, D. C. (1999). The impact of psychological contract violations on exit, voice, loyalty, and neglect. *Human Relations.* 52(7), 895–922.

Vancouver, J. B. and Schmitt, N. W. (1991). An exploratory examination of person-organization fit: Organizational goal congruence. *Personnel Psychology.* 44, 333–352.

Wagner, J. A., III (1995). Studies of individualism-collectivism: Effects on cooperation in groups. *Academy of Management Journal.* 38(1), 152–172.

Watanabe, N. and Takahashi, K. (1999). Spurious loyalty of Japanese Workers. In search of psychodynamics of substitutive mother in the form of organization. Available at www.isposia/Symposia/Toronto/1999wantanable-takahashi.htm.

Wehling, J. and Scholl, W. (1993). Dissatisfied employees — Causes and reactions, and interdisciplinary approach in the exit-voice tradition. Dissertation. Goettingen University (in German).

Whitener, E. M. and Walz, P. M. (1993). Exchange theory determinants of affective and continuance commitment and turnover. *Journal of Vocational Behavior*. 42, 265–281.

Williamson, O. E. (1975). *Markets and Hierarchies: Analysis and Antitrust Implications*. New York: Free Press.

Williamson, O. E. (1991a). Comparative economic organization: The analysis of discrete structural alternatives. *Administrative Science Quarterly*. 36, 269–296.

Williamson, O. E. (1991b). Strategizing, economizing, and economic organization. *Strategic Management Journal*. 13, 483–498.

Withey, M. J. and Cooper, W. H. (1989). Predicting exit, voice, loyalty, and neglect. *Administrative Science Quarterly*. 34(4), 521–539.

Zahavi, A. (1975). Mate selection — A selection for a handicap. *Journal of Theoretical Biology*. 53(1), 205–214.

Zangaro, G. A. (2001). Organizational commitment: A concept analysis. *Nursing Forum*. 36(2), 14–22.

Index

absence behavior, 22
absenteeism, 2, 22, 23, 30
active negative commitment, 10
active positive commitment, 10
active voice, 52
affective, 4, 10, 41
affective commitment, 22
Affective Commitment Scale, 15
age, 62
agency employment, 6, 35
alienated involvement, 3
alienation, 3
altruism, 18, 72
altruistic behavior, 69
attachment, 3
atypical, 35
atypical work arrangements, 6, 37

behaviorally committed employees, 74
behavioral modes of commitment, 43
behavioral organizational commitment (BOC), 38–43, 46–48, 51, 52, 54, 55, 57, 60, 61, 72, 73, 75

BOC forms, 41–43, 56
BOC scale, 50, 72
extreme unrewarded BOC, 40
negative BOC, 52
positive BOC, 52
rewarded BOC, 40, 63, 65
unrewarded (Sisyphean) BOC, 39, 40, 42, 57, 61, 65, 75

calculative-instrumental, 3
calculative involvement, 3
civic virtue, 18
commitment, ix, xi, xii, 6, 19, 22, 28, 30, 31, 40, 49, 69
commitment behavior, 37, 40, 44
commitment declaration, 68
commitment modes, 54
commitment phenomenon, 59
commitment scale, 45
committed person, 40
compliance, 3
concrete commitment, 31
conscientiousness, 18
constructive commitment, 48
continuance, 3, 4, 10, 33

85

Printed in the United States
By Bookmasters